ughton
fflin
rcourt

PERFORMANCE ASSESSMENT

10

Approaching Performance Assessments with Confidence

By Carol Jago

In order to get good at anything, you need to practice. Whether the goal is to improve your jump shot, level up in a video game, or make the cut in band tryouts, success requires repeated practice on the court, computer, and field. The same is true of reading and writing. The only way to get good at them is by reading and writing.

Malcolm Gladwell estimates in his book *Outliers* that mastering a skill requires about 10,000 hours of dedicated practice. He argues that individuals who are outstanding in their field have one thing in common—many, many hours of working at it. Gladwell claims that success is less dependent on innate talent than it is on practice. Now I'm pretty sure that I could put in 10,000 hours at a ballet studio and still be a terrible dancer, but I agree with Gladwell that, "Practice isn't the thing you do once you're good. It's the thing you do that makes you good."

Not just any kind of practice will help you master a skill, though. Effective practice needs to focus on improvement. That is why this series of reading and writing tasks begins with a model of the kind of reading and writing you are working towards, then takes you through practice exercises, and finally invites you to perform the skills you have practiced.

Once through the cycle is only the beginning. You will want to repeat the process many times over until close reading, supporting claims with evidence, and crafting a compelling essay is something you approach with confidence. Notice that I didn't say "with ease." I wish it were otherwise, but in my experience as a teacher and as an author, writing well is never easy.

The work is worth the effort. Like a star walking out on the stage, you put your trust in the hours you've invested in practice to result in thundering applause. To our work together!

Unit 1 Argumentative Essay
Big Issues

STEP 1 ANALYZE THE MODEL

Should high school start an hour later?

Read Source Materials

STEP 2 PRACTICE THE TASK

Should a business have the right to ban teenagers?

Read Source Materials

Write an Argumentative Essay

STEP 3 PERFORM THE TASK

Should the minimum driving age be raised?

Read Source Materials

Unit 2 Informative Essay
Great Adaptations

STEP 1 ANALYZE THE MODEL

How have birds and lizards adapted to their environments?

Read Source Materials

STEP 2 PRACTICE THE TASK

What adaptations allow deep-sea creatures to survive in extreme environments? Why do they need these adaptations?

Read Source Materials

Write an Informative Essay

STEP 3 PERFORM THE TASK

How have Australian animals adapted to their environment?

Read Source Materials

Write an Informative Essay

Unit 3 Literary Analysis
Inspirations

STEP 1 ANALYZE THE MODEL

What inspires us to grow and change?

Read Source Materials

STEP 2 PRACTICE THE TASK

How can real events inspire poetry?

Read Source Materials

STEP 3 PERFORM THE TASK

How can inspiration sustain us in difficult times?

Read Source Materials

© Houghton Mifflin Harcourt Publishing Company • Image Credits: ©Creativemarc/Shutterstock; ©Houghton Mifflin Harcourt; ©Creativa/Shutterstock

Unit 4 Mixed Practice
On Your Own

© Houghton Mifflin Harcourt Publishing Company

Big Issues

Argumentative Essay

1 ANALYZE THE MODEL

Evaluate an argumentative essay that offers reasons why high school should or should not begin later in the day.

2 PRACTICE THE TASK

Write an argumentative essay that offers reasons for or against a business's right to ban teenagers from its establishment.

3 PERFORM THE TASK

Write an argumentative essay that offers reasons for or against raising the minimum driving age.

How do we relate to and interact with other people—friends, enemies, neighbors, strangers, and those with whom we disagree? And how does age affect the way that people act or react in difficult or controversial situations?

No doubt you have been involved in many arguments—squabbles with your friends, disagreements with siblings, and those times when you have tried to convince someone about something you want. This kind of informal, conversational give-and-take is different from a formal argument.

IN THIS UNIT, you will learn how to write an argumentative essay that is based on your close reading and analysis of several relevant sources. You will learn a step-by-step approach to stating a claim, and then organize your essay to support your claim in a clear and logical way.

Should high school start an hour later?

You will read:

▶ **TWO INFORMATIONAL ARTICLES**
from Sleep Deprivation in Teenagers

from School Start Time and Sleep

You will analyze:

▶ **A STUDENT MODEL**
We Need Our Sleep!

Source Materials for Step 1

The texts on these two pages were used by Mr. Louie's student, Jon Attridge, as sources for his essay, *"We Need Our Sleep!"* As you read, make notes in the side columns and underline information that you find useful.

NOTES

from

Sleep Deprivation in Teenagers

Medical Journal Today

For the past 30 years, Dr. Smith and his research team have studied sleep patterns in high school students. These studies of 14 to 18-year-olds have shown that when students learn something new and are then deprived of REM sleep, their test scores go down dramatically. This comes as no surprise to Dr. Smith, who knows that certain kinds of memory are sensitive to sleep loss. He theorizes that, if 14 to 18-year-olds are susceptible to such affects when prevented from getting enough sleep, younger children might be affected more severely. Students in grade school need between 9 and 10 hours of sleep for optimal learning.

Although it may vary from person to person, most teenagers need 9.5 hours of sleep. Unfortunately, extracurricular activities, after-school jobs, and homework may result in teenagers getting no more than 7.5 hours of sleep a night. If teens consistently do not get enough sleep, their moods can be affected. They will have difficulty performing and reacting as usual.

from
School Start Time and Sleep

National Sleep Foundation

NOTES

"Early to bed, early to rise makes a man healthy, wealthy and wise," said Ben Franklin. But does this adage apply to teenagers? Research in the 1990s found that later sleep and wake patterns among adolescents are biologically determined; the natural tendency for teenagers is to stay up late at night and wake up later in the morning. This research indicates that school bells that ring as early as 7:00 a.m. in many parts of the country stand in stark contrast with adolescents' sleep patterns and needs.

Evidence suggests that teenagers are indeed seriously sleep deprived. A recent poll conducted by the National Sleep Foundation found that 60% of children under the age of 18 complained of being tired during the day, according to their parents, and 15% said they fell asleep at school during the year.

On April 2, 1999, Rep. Zoe Lofgren (D-CA), introduced a congressional resolution to encourage schools and school districts to reconsider early morning start times to be more in sync with teens' biological makeup. House Congressional Resolution 135 or the "ZZZ's to A's" Act would encourage individual schools and school districts all over the country to move school start times to no earlier than 8:30 a.m.

Discuss and Decide

You have read two sources about teenagers and sleep. Without going any farther, discuss the question: Should high school start an hour later each morning?

Analyze a Student Model for Step 1

Read Jon's argumentative essay closely. The red side notes are the comments that his teacher, Mr. Louie, wrote.

Jon Attridge
Mr. Louie
English 10
October 28

We Need Our Sleep!

Nice hook. The issue and your claim are both clear. Your audience is clear.

Beep! You shut off the alarm. It's 6:00 A.M.—time to get ready for school, but you don't have the energy. According to a recent study, 85% of teens in America aren't getting the sleep they need. So you, like most of the teens in America, aren't getting the sleep you need. Is this the morning you want to experience for the rest of your school career? No. School should start later.

Good paragraph.

Logical follow-up to your introduction. Valid reason, well-supported by sufficient evidence.

Getting up too early has serious consequences. Studies from the American Psychological Association show that the frontal lobe (the section of the brain in charge of learning ability and memory) is still developing in many adolescents. Disturbing REM (rapid eye movement) sleep can slow the development of this vital portion of the brain. This can result in much lower test scores. Our principal said, "Students in first period classes tend to score lower on standardized math tests than their peers who take the same classes later in the day." We should be as concerned about disturbing students' natural sleep patterns as we are about skipping school.

Moreover, Trent University studies on sleep deprivation have shown that grades aren't the only thing that might improve. An additional hour of sleep can positively affect a student's mood and attitude. My grandfather says that when he was in school, students went to school later and were better rested. With students' moods boosted, teachers and students would get along in stress-free situations.

Some may argue that teenagers should simply adapt—go to bed earlier or otherwise adjust to the reality of an early school day. I refer them to research done in the 1990s, which found that later sleep and wake patterns in adolescents are biologically determined. Experts talked, and California Representative Zoe Lofgren listened. She introduced House Congressional Resolution 135, the "ZZZ's to A's Act," to encourage schools to start no earlier than 8:30 A.M.

Now imagine that morning again. It's 7:00 A.M. You say to yourself, "Wow, I feel great, and I've got plenty of time to get ready." Just one hour can make a huge difference in your mood and your day.

You use an effective transition to create cohesion and signal the introduction of another reason. Your language is formal and non-combative. You remain focused on your purpose.

You anticipated and addressed an opposing claim that is likely to occur to your audience. Your answer to the opposing claim is well-supported with valid evidence.

Smooth flow from beginning to end. Clear conclusion restates your claim. Your evidence is convincing. Excellent use of conventions of English. Good job!

Discuss and Decide

Did Jon convince you that school should start an hour later? If so, which evidence was the most compelling?

Terminology of Argumentative Texts

Read each term and explanation. Then look back at Jon Attridge's argumentative essay and find an example to complete the chart.

Term	Explanation	Example from Jon's Essay
audience	The **audience** for your argument is a group of people that you want to convince. As you develop your argument, consider your audience's knowledge level and concerns.	
purpose	The **purpose** for writing an argument is to sway the audience. Your purpose should be clear, whether it is to persuade your audience to agree with your claim, or to motivate your audience to take some action.	
precise claim	A **precise claim** confidently states your viewpoint. Remember that you must be able to find reasons and evidence to support your claim, and that you must distinguish your claim from opposing claims.	
reason	A **reason** is a statement that supports your claim. (You should have more than one reason.) Note that you will need to supply evidence for each reason you state.	
opposing claim	An **opposing claim**, or **counterclaim,** shares the point of view of people who do not agree with your claim. Opposing claims must be fairly presented with evidence.	

PRACTICE THE TASK

Should a business have the right to ban teenagers?

You will read:

▶ **A NEWSPAPER AD**
Munchy's Promise

▶ **A BUSINESS ANALYSIS**
Munchy's Patrons, July and October
Munchy's Monthly Sales,
July–October

▶ **A STUDENT BLOG**
Munchy's Bans Students!

▶ **A NEWSPAPER EDITORIAL**
A Smart Idea Can Save a Business

You will write:

▶ **AN ARGUMENTATIVE ESSAY**
Should a business have the right to ban teenagers?

Source Materials for Step 2

AS YOU READ Analyze the ad, business analysis, blog, and editorial. Think about the information, including the data contained in the sources. Annotate the sources with notes that help you decide where you stand on the issue: Should a business have the right to ban teenagers?

Source 1: Newspaper Ad

Munchy's Promise

Aren't you tired of eating lunch surrounded by noisy high school students?

Aren't you fed up with endless cellphone conversations, loud music, messy tables?

Aren't you infuriated seeing teenage students taking over every restaurant downtown?

We promise that you'll have the quiet lunch you deserve, because MUNCHY's has the solution!

No music!
No cellphones!
NO STUDENTS!

Mr. Joe "Munchy" Jones and his team will make sure you get the midday break that YOU deserve!

Munchy's
321 Main Street
555-5252

Use this coupon for a **10% discount** on your next "quiet lunch."

COME TO A "QUIET LUNCH" AT MUNCHY'S!
From noon to 3 pm, Monday through Friday, we will be a teen-free zone!

Close Read

1. What assumptions is Mr. Jones making about teenagers?

_____

2. What assumptions is he making about adults?

_____

Source 2: Business Analysis

Mr. Jones,
Here is the analysis of July vs. October data.
Your Accountant,
Hector Ramirez, CPA

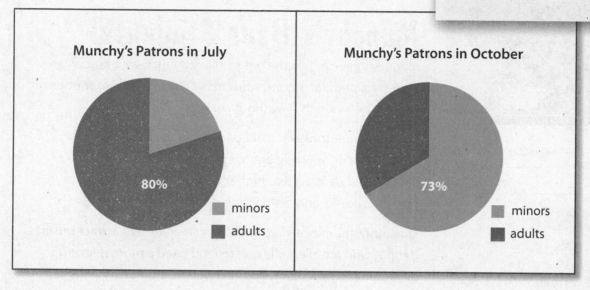

Munchy's Patrons in July

80%

minors
adults

Munchy's Patrons in October

73%

minors
adults

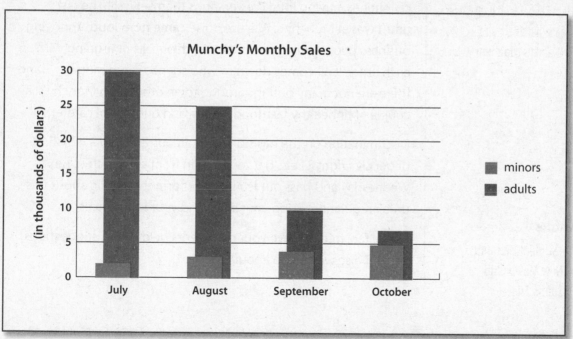

Munchy's Monthly Sales

(in thousands of dollars)

30
25
20
15
10
5
0

July   August   September   October

minors
adults

Discuss and Decide

1. Explain the data shown in the pie charts.

2. What is the implication of the data shown in the bar graph?

3. Explain the relationship between the two forms of data.

Source 3: Student Blog

Enter your email address:

Subscribe me!

Profile

This blog is run by the Student Council of Springfield High School, and it discusses issues and events that affect all the students of SHS and its community.

Labels

unfair
high school
students
lunch
action

Previous entries

November 15

👍 Like   👎 Dislike

Munchy's Bans Students!

In today's newspaper, the old-fashioned lunch spot known as Munchy's, popular among students of this institution, announced its new "quiet lunch"—without students!

The restaurant took out a full-page ad in the newspaper to advertise its new rule banning students from noon to 3 P.M. The ad claimed that high school students are noisy, play loud music, and are on their cellphones all the time.

Obviously, this piece of advertising was crafted to attract business people, who are allegedly quieter and need a more relaxing environment. Newsflash! Business people are ALWAYS on their cellphones, having loud converstions themselves!!! The last time I was at Munchy's, ALL the noise came from loud, annoying business people who were either on their cells or arguing with each other. It all comes down to who spends more money . . . and there are not many options around town other than Munchy's: a couple of unhealthy fast-food places, and our school cafeteria.

Discrimination on the basis of age is an outrage and a violation of our civil rights! Let's get together in front of Munchy's next Wednesday and pass out leaflets to inform the public about this unfair regulation. Bring your signs and your loud voices!

Please feel free to leave your comments below with suggestions of what else we can do about this.

Close Read

Does the lunch hour ban on teens guarantee a "quiet lunch"? Cite evidence in the blog text to support your answer.

Source 4: Newspaper Editorial

Springfield Daily Mail

A Smart Idea Can Save a Business

November 17

In these days of economic uncertainty, the last thing business owners want to do is drive customers away. We are witnessing the hardships that many local stores and restaurants are facing in our city, fighting to at least break even and stay open. In order to reinvigorate the economy, the Mayor herself has pointed out the relationship between a thriving business district and property values. This issue affects us all. The Mayor's office is trying to attract more people downtown by investing in making the streets more beautiful, converting areas to pedestrian-only zones, and giving business owners some tax breaks if they help promote the city's tourist attractions.

But most of the time, municipal help is not enough, and rather than hang a "going out of business" sign on their front door, some business owners try to take the bull by the horns and make their own rules in order to improve their revenue.

This week, we applaud the marketing strategy of Joseph Jones, who took out a full-page ad announcing a policy change at Munchy's, his popular eatery. After identifying a decrease in profits during the school months, Mr. Jones realized that many of his faithful, adult, wealthier, customers—mostly business people from the offices that surround his restaurant downtown—were staying away from Munchy's due to the havoc high school students cause every day at lunchtime. In fact, teens are to a restaurant like weeds are to a garden. Therefore, he proclaimed the hours between noon and 3 P.M. "quiet lunch" time, during which students will be banned from the premises. This regulation will encourage business people—who spend more money on their lunches and need a peaceful break from their busy days—back into the restaurant.

We wish Mr. Jones and the team at Munchy's the best of luck, and we congratulate them once more for their creative idea!

Discuss and Decide

1. What smart idea does the editorial applaud?
2. What reasons are given to endorse Mr. Jones' new policy?

Respond to Questions on Step 2 Sources

These questions will help you analyze the sources you've read. Use your notes and refer to the sources in order to answer the questions. Your answers to these questions will help you write your essay.

1 Evaluate the sources. Is the evidence from one source more credible than the evidence from another source? When you evaluate the credibility of a source, examine the expertise of the author and/or the organization responsible for the information. Record your reasons in the chart.

Source	Credible?	Reasons
Newspaper Ad Munchy's Promise		
Business Analysis		
Student Blog Munchy's Bans Students!		
Newspaper Editorial A Smart Idea Can Save a Business		

2 **Prose Constructed-Response** If you were supportive of "Munchy" Jones' position, which sources would you use to defend your opinion? Explain your rationale, citing evidence from the sources.

_____

_____

3 **Prose Constructed-Response** Examine the data in the Business Analysis. Explain to what extent the blog and the newspaper editorial could rely on or use these data.

_____

_____

Types of Evidence

Every reason you offer to support the central claim of your argument must be upheld by evidence. It is useful to think ahead about evidence when you are preparing to write an argument. If the evidence to support your claim, is limited or unconvincing, you will need to revise your claim. The evidence you provide must be relevant, or related to your claim. It must also be sufficient. Sufficient evidence is both clear and varied.

Use this chart to help you vary the types of evidence you provide to support your reasons.

Types of Evidence	What Does It Look Like?
Anecdotes: personal examples or stories that illustrate a point	**Blog** "The last time I was at Munchy's, ALL the noise came from loud, annoying business people who were either on their cells or arguing with each other."
Commonly accepted beliefs: ideas that most people share	**Newspaper Ad** ". . . noisy high school students."
Examples: specific instances or illustrations of a general idea	**Blog** ". . . there are not many options around town other than Munchy's: a couple of unhealthy fast-food places . . ."
Expert opinion: statement made by an authority on the subject	**Editorial** . . . The Mayor herself has pointed out the relationship between a thriving business and property values. . . .
Facts: statements that can be proven true, such as statistics or other numerical information	**Business Analysis** Adults spent $30,000 at Munchy's in July.

Planning and Prewriting

Before you draft your essay, complete some important planning steps.

Claim ➡ Reasons ➡ Evidence

 You may prefer to do your planning on a computer.

Make a Precise Claim

1. Do you agree or disagree with Munchy's? That is, should a business have the right to ban teenagers?　　　yes ☐　　no ☐

2. Review the evidence on pages 10–13. Do the sources support your position?　　　yes ☐　　no ☐

3. If you answered *no* to Question 2, you can either change your position or do additional research to find supporting evidence.

4. State your claim. It should be precise. It should contain the issue and your position on the issue.

Issue: Should a business have the right to ban teenagers?

Your position on the issue: _____

Your precise claim: _____

State Reasons

Next gather support for your claim. Identify several valid reasons that justify your position.

Reason 1	Reason 2	Reason 3

Find Evidence

You have identified reasons that support your claim. Summarize your reasons in the chart below. Then complete the chart by identifying evidence that supports your reasons.

Relevant Evidence: The evidence you plan to use must be *relevant* to your argument. That is, it should directly and factually support your position.

Sufficient Evidence: Additionally, your evidence must be *sufficient* to make your case. That is, you need to supply enough evidence to convince others

Short Summary of Reasons	Evidence
Reason 1	Relevant? _____ Sufficient? _____
Reason 2	Relevant? _____ Sufficient? _____
Reason 3	Relevant? _____ Sufficient? _____

Finalize Your Plan

Whether you are writing your essay at home or working in a timed situation at school, it is important to have a plan. You will save time and create a more organized, logical essay by planning the structure before you start writing.

Use your responses on pages 16–17, as well as your close reading notes, to complete the graphic organizer.

▶ Think about how you will grab your reader's attention with an interesting fact or anecdote.

▶ Identify the issue and your position.

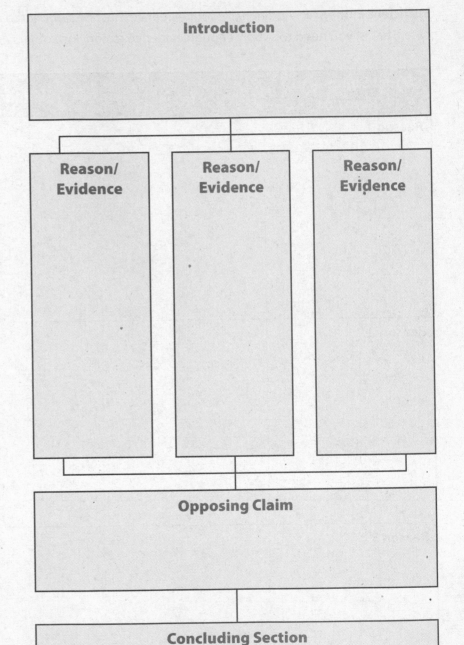

▶ State your precise claim.
▶ List the likely opposing claim and how you will counter it.

▶ Restate your claim.

Draft Your Essay

As you write, think about:

▶ **Audience:** Your teacher

▶ **Purpose:** Demonstrate your understanding of the specific requirements of an argumentative essay.

▶ **Style:** Use a formal and objective tone that isn't defensive.

▶ **Transitions:** Use words, such as *furthermore* or *another reason* to create cohesion, or flow.

Revise

Revision Checklist: Self Evaluation

Use the checklist below to analyze your writing.

 If you drafted your essay on the computer, you may wish to print it out so that you can more easily evaluate it.

Ask Yourself	Tips	Revision Strategies
Does the introduction grab the audience's attention and include a precise claim?	Draw a wavy line under the attention-grabbing text. Bracket the claim.	Add an attention grabber. Add a claim or rework the existing one to make it more precise.
Do at least two valid reasons support the claim? Is each reason supported by relevant and sufficient evidence?	Underline each reason. Circle each piece of evidence, and draw an arrow to the reason it supports.	Add reasons or revise existing ones to make them more valid. Add relevant evidence to ensure that your support is sufficient.
Do transitions create cohesion and link related parts of the argument?	Put a star next to each transition.	Add words, phrases, or clauses to connect related ideas that lack transitions.
Are the reasons in the order that is most persuasive?	Number the reasons in the margin, ranking them by their strength and effectiveness.	Rearrange the reasons into a more logical order of importance.
Are opposing claims fairly acknowledged and refuted?	Put a plus sign by any sentence that addresses an opposing claim.	Add sentences that identify and address those opposing claims.
Does the concluding section restate the claim?	Put a box around the restatement of your claim.	Add a sentence that restates your claim.

Revision Checklist: Peer Review

Exchange your essay with a classmate, or read it aloud to your partner. As you read and comment on your classmate's essay, focus on logic, organization, and evidence—not on whether you agree with the author's claim. Help each other identify parts of the draft that need strengthening, reworking, or a new approach.

What To Look For	Notes for My Partner
1. Does the introduction grab the audience's attention and include a precise claim?	
2. Do at least two valid reasons support the claim? Is each reason supported by relevant and sufficient evidence?	
3. Do transitions create cohesion and link related parts of the argument?	
4. Are the reasons in the order that is most persuasive?	
5. Are opposing claims fairly acknowledged and refuted?	
6. Does the concluding section restate the claim?	

Edit

 Edit your essay to correct spelling, grammar, and punctuation errors.

Should the minimum driving age be raised?

You will read:

▶ **TWO INFORMATIONAL ARTICLES**

Traffic Safety Facts

Teenage Driving Laws May Just Delay Deadly Crashes

You will write:

▶ **AN ARGUMENTATIVE ESSAY**

Should the minimum driving age be raised?

Part 1: Read Sources
Source 1: Informational Article

2008 Data

TRAFFIC SAFETY FACTS

from the National Highway Traffic Safety Administration (NHTSA)

AS YOU READ *Analyze the data presented in the articles. Look for evidence that supports your position on the dangers of too much online time, or evidence that inspires you to change your position.*

NOTES

There were 205.7 million licensed drivers in the United States in 2007 (2008 data not available). Young drivers, between 15 and 20 years old, accounted for 6.4 percent (13.2 million) of the total, a 4.8-percent increase from the 12.6 million young drivers in 1997. In 2008, 5,864 15- to 20-year-old drivers were involved in fatal crashes—a 27-percent decrease from the 7,987 involved in 1998. Driver fatalities for this age group decreased by 20 percent between 1998 and 2008. For young males, driver fatalities decreased by 19 percent, compared with a 24-percent decrease for young females
10 (Table 1). Motor vehicle crashes are the leading cause of death for 15- to 20-year-olds (based on 2005 figures, which are the latest mortality data currently available from the National Center for Health Statistics). In 2008, 2,739 15- to 20-year-old drivers were killed and an additional 228,000 were injured in motor vehicle crashes.

Close Read

How many fewer 15- to 20-year-old drivers were involved in fatal crashes in 2008 than in 1998? Cite textual evidence in your response.

_____

_____

_____

1. Analyze   2. Practice   3. Perform

Graph

Driver Fatalities and Drivers Involved in Fatal Crashes Among 15- to 20- Year Old Drivers, 1998–2008

Number of Drivers

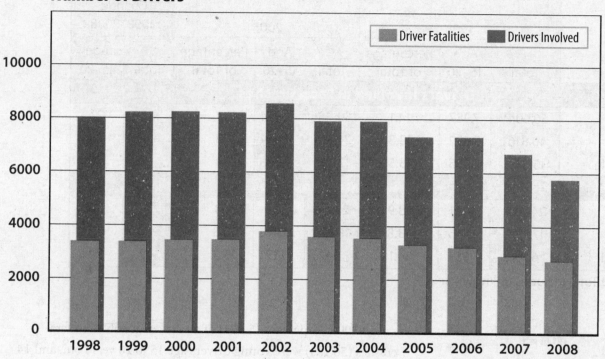

Close Read

Is this a true statement? *In 2002, more than half of fatal crashes among 15- to 20-year-olds killed someone other than the driver.* Use the data in the graph and cite evidence in your response.

_____

_____

_____

Table 1

Involvement of 15- to 20-Year Old Drivers in Fatal Crashes by Sex, 1998 and 2008

	1998			2008			Percentage Change, 1998–2008	
	Total	Age 15–20	Percentage of Total	Total	Age 15–20	Percentage of Total	Total	Age 15–20
Drivers Involved in Fatal Crashes								
Total	56,604	7,987	14.1	50, 186	5,864	11.7	-11	-27
Male	40,816	5,652	13.8	36,881	4,174	11.3	-10	-26
Female	15,089	2,335	15.5	12,568	1,688	13.4	-17	-28
Driver Fatalitites								
Total	24,743	3,431	13.9	24,175	2,739	11.3	- 2	-20
Male	17,992	2,476	13.8	18,694	2,010	10.8	- 4	-19
Female	6,750	955	14.1	5,473	727	13.3	-19	-24

Note: Total includes unknown sex.

NOTES

In 2008, 12 percent (5,864) of all drivers involved in fatal crashes (50,186) were young drivers age 15 to 20 years old, and 14 percent (1,429,000) of all drivers involved in police-reported crashes (10,081,000) were young drivers.

Close Read

What can you conclude about the behavior of male and female drivers? What other factors could explain the difference?

_____

_____

_____

_____

1. Analyze   2. Practice   3. Perform

Table 2

Population and Drivers Involved in Fatal Crashes by Age Group, 2008

	Age Group (Years)							
	15–20	21–24	25–34	35–44	45–54	55–64	65–69	70+
Population (Percent)	8.5	5.5	13.5	14.0	14.6	11.1	3.7	9.1
Drivers Involved in Fatal Crashes (Percent)								
–Single-Vehicle	14.0	13.1	20.9	16.9	15.5	10.3	2.8	6.2
–Multi-Vehicle	10.4	9.2	19.0	18.3	17.8	12.4	3.5	9.3
–All Fatal Crashes	11.9	10.8	19.8	17.8	16.8	11.5	3.2	8.1

Among 15- to 20-year-old drivers involved in fatal crashes in
20 2008, 30 percent (291) of those who did not have valid operator's licenses at the time of the crash also had previous license suspensions or revocations (Table 3).

Table 3

Young Drivers Involved in Fatal Crashes by Previous Driving Record and License Compliance, 2008

	License Compliance				Total (5,864)*	
	Valid (4,882)		Invalid (970)			
Driving Record	Number	Percent	Number	Percent	Number	Percent
Previous Recorded Crashes	748	15.5	96	9.9	845	14.4
Previous Recorded Suspensions and Revocations	433	9.0	291	30.0	727	12.4
Previous DWI Convictions	63	1.3	37	3.8	100	1.7
Previous Speeding Convictions	1,017	21.1	135	13.9	1,154	19.7
Previous Other Harmful or Moving Convictions	877	18.2	182	18.8	1,060	18.1

* Includes 72 drivers with unknown license status. Note: Excluding all drivers with unknown previous records.

Close Read

Cite evidence from the text and graphics to support this statement: *Driver fatalities for 15- to 20-year-olds decreased 20% between 1998 and 2008.*

SEPTEMBER 14

Teenage Driving Laws
May Just Delay Deadly Crashes

by Anahad O'Connor

AS YOU READ *Pay attention to cause-and-effect relationships between changing licensing laws for teenage drivers and the rate of fatal crashes. Jot down comments or questions about the text in the side margins.*

NOTES

A nationwide study shows that tougher licensing laws for teenage drivers have reduced deadly accidents among 16-year-olds, but with an unintended consequence: increasing the fatal crash rate among 18-year-olds.

Over the last two decades, many states have put in place strict teenage driving laws, with graduated driver's license programs that require young drivers to meet certain restrictions before they obtain a full license. While the rules vary by state, they generally set a minimum age for earning a driver's permit or license and require a 10 set number of supervised hours behind the wheel, and some prohibit driving with fellow teenagers, ban night driving or require at least six months of instruction before a driver's test. Over all, the tougher laws—which most states began adopting in the mid-1990s—have been credited with a 30 percent drop in highway fatalities among teenagers.

But "most of the prior studies on graduated driver licensing have only looked at 16-year-olds," said Scott Masten, a researcher with California's Department of Motor Vehicles and the lead author of the current study. "When you do that you go, 'Wow, these programs are 20 saving lives,'" he said.

Discuss and Decide

Before reading the rest of the selection, discuss what sorts of reasons could account for the phenomenon mentioned in the first paragraph.

To get a broader perspective, Dr. Masten and his colleagues looked at data on fatal crashes involving 16- to 19-year-olds that occurred over a 21-year period, beginning in 1986. "When you look at the bigger picture across 18- and 19-year-olds, it looks like we're offsetting those saved crashes," he said. "In fact, 75 percent of the fatal crashes we thought we were saving actually just occurred two years later. It's shocking."

The study, published Wednesday in The Journal of the American Medical Association, found that since the first graduated driver programs were instituted, there have been 1,348 fewer deadly crashes involving 16-year-old drivers. But at the same time, there have been 1,086 more fatal crashes that involved 18-year-olds. The net difference is still an improvement, Dr. Masten said, but not quite the effect that many had assumed.

"The bottom line is there is still a net overall savings from introducing all these programs," he said. "So we are saving teen drivers over all, but it's not nearly what we thought it would be."

Dr. Masten strongly suspects that the reason for the increase in deadly crashes among 18-year-olds is that many teenagers, rather than deal with the extra restrictions for 16- and 17-year-olds, are simply waiting to get a license until they turn 18, and skipping the restrictions altogether. As a result, a greater proportion of inexperienced drivers hit the road at 18. He pointed out that when California instituted its tougher driving laws for teenagers, the proportion of 16- and 17-year-olds getting licenses to drive dropped while the numbers at 18 and 19 did not.

But the authors also suggested another hypothesis: that teenagers going through graduated driver license programs are not getting as much practical driving experience when they have "co-drivers." In other words, while having adult supervision in the car reduces risk, it also protects teenage drivers so much that they miss out on learning experiences that can be gleaned only by driving alone, like knowing what it means to be fully responsible for a vehicle and knowing how to "self-regulate."

Discuss and Decide

How have teenage driving laws changed? Cite textual evidence in your response.

"Even though we want you to learn by driving with your parents, it's really different from the sorts of things you learn when you're driving on your own," Dr. Masten said. "The whole thing about learning to drive is you need to expose yourself to crash risk to get experience."

60   In an editorial that accompanied the study, researchers with the Insurance Institute for Highway Safety, a nonprofit group financed by insurance companies, said the findings raised a "serious issue" that policy makers should take note of. They pointed out that one of the states with the toughest programs for teenage drivers is New Jersey, where all first-time drivers under 21 have to adhere to graduated driver restrictions.

"New Jersey's approach has been associated with significant reductions in the crash rates for 17- and 18-year-olds and virtually eliminates crashes among 16-year-olds, without adversely affecting

70   crash rates for 19-year-old drivers," the authors wrote.

But in a twist, New Jersey's tough laws may have just shifted the effect to 21-year-olds, similar to the way tough restrictions on 16- and 17-year-olds were followed by a spike in deadly crashes among 18-year-olds in other states, Dr. Masten said. In New Jersey, a study of deadly crashes did not look specifically at 21-year-olds; they were mixed into a larger group of 20- to 24-year-olds. But the research still found a 10 percent increase in deadly crashes in that group after New Jersey's tougher graduated driver licensing program was instituted, suggesting that 18-, 19- and 20-year-olds may be waiting out the

80   tough restrictions there as well.

Close Read

What general principle does New Jersey's experience suggest about driving restrictions and age?

_____

_____

_____

1. Analyze   2. Practice   3. Perform

Other researchers have also found that the reason the rate of crashes among teenagers is so high—they account for 10 times as many crashes as middle-aged drivers—is not that they are reckless, but that they make simple mistakes, like failing to scan the road, misjudging driving conditions and becoming distracted. Some of these problems can be addressed through what experts call narrative driving: having adult drivers point out to teenage passengers examples of unsafe driving and explain to them how they are dealing with distractions on the road.

90   Lack of sleep can also be a major factor in teenage crashes. A study in the Journal of Clinical Sleep Medicine this year found that teenagers who started school earlier in the morning had higher crash rates.

Close Read

Provide evidence from the article that supports the position of allowing teenagers to drive at age 16. Then provide evidence that supports the position of *not* allowing teenagers to drive at 16.

Pro	Con
Support Allowing 16-Year-Olds to Drive	**Against Allowing 16-Year-Olds to Drive**

Respond to Questions on Step 3 Sources

These questions will help you think about the sources you've read. Use your notes and refer to the sources in order to answer the questions. Your answers to these questions will help you write your essay.

1 Is the evidence from one source more credible than the evidence from another source? When you evaluate the credibility of a source, examine the expertise of the author and/or the organization responsible for the information. Record your reasons.

Source	Credible?	Reasons
Informational Article Traffic Saftey Facts		
Informational Article Teenage Driving Laws May Just Delay Deadly Crashes		

2 **Prose Constructed-Response** What point about teen driving is raised in both the blog "Teenage Driving Laws May Just Delay Deadly Crashes" and the data from "Traffic Safety Facts"? Why is this point important to address when making an informed decision about teen driving? Support your answer with details and statistics.

_____

_____

_____

3 **Prose Constructed-Response** Does the bar graph in "Traffic Safety Facts" support or contradict the information in the article "Teenage Driving Laws May Just Delay Deadly Crashes"? Use details from the article and the graph to support your answer.

_____

_____

_____

Part 2: Write

ASSIGNMENT

You have read about traffic accidents caused by teens. Now write an argumentative essay answering the question: Should the minimum driving age be raised? Support your claim with details from what you have read.

Plan

Use the graphic organizer to help you outline the structure of your argumentative essay.

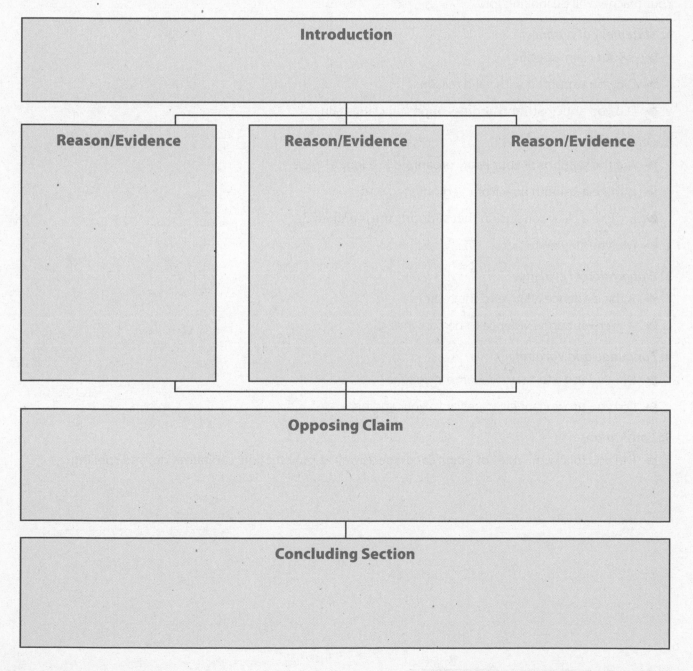

Introduction

Reason/Evidence

Reason/Evidence

Reason/Evidence

Opposing Claim

Concluding Section

Draft

 Use your notes and completed graphic organizer to write a first draft of your argumentative essay.

Revise and Edit

 Look back over your essay and compare it to the Evaluation Criteria. Revise your essay and edit it to correct spelling, grammar, and punctuation errors.

Evaluation Criteria

Your teacher will be looking for:

1. *Statement of purpose*

▶ Is your claim specific?

▶ Did you support it with valid reasons?

▶ Did you anticipate and address opposing claims fairly?

2. *Organization*

▶ Are the sections of your essay organized in a logical way?

▶ Is there a smooth flow from beginning to end?

▶ Is there a clear conclusion that supports the argument?

▶ Did you stay on topic?

3. *Elaboration of evidence*

▶ Is the evidence relative to the topic?

▶ Is there enough evidence to be convincing?

4. *Language and Vocabulary*

▶ Did you use a formal, noncombative tone?

▶ Did you use vocabulary familiar to your audience?

5. *Conventions*

▶ Did you follow the rules of grammar usage as well as punctuation, capitalization, and spelling?

Great Adaptations

Informative Essay

© Houghton Mifflin Harcourt Publishing Company

STEP 1

ANALYZE THE MODELS

Evaluate two informative essays. The first is about the albatross and the cormorant, and the second is about winged lizards.

STEP 2

PRACTICE THE TASK

Write an informative essay about deep-sea creatures.

STEP 3

PERFORM THE TASK

Write an informative essay on adaptations made by wildlife in Australia.

An informative essay, also called an expository essay, is a short work of nonfiction that informs and explains. Unlike fiction, nonfiction is mainly written to convey factual information, although writers of nonfiction shape information in a way that matches their own purposes. Nonfiction writing can be found in newspaper, magazine, and online articles, as well as in biographies, speeches, movie and book reviews, and truelife adventure stories.

The nonfiction topics that you will read about in this unit describe animals in very different environments. The information in the sources is factual.

IN THIS UNIT, you will analyze information from two articles on native and invasive new animals in Australia. You will select and organize relevant facts and ideas to convey information about a topic, and you will end your essay by summarizing ideas or providing a concluding statement.

ANALYZE THE MODEL

How have birds and lizards adapted to their environments?

You will read:

▶ **AN INFORMATIONAL ARTICLE**
Don't Start Without a Plan

You will analyze:

▶ **TWO STUDENT MODELS**
Two Water Birds: The Albatross and the Cormorant

Winged Lizards

Source Materials for Step 1

Mr. Sullivan's students read the following text to help them plan and write an informative essay. As you read, underline information that you find useful.

NOTES

Don't Start Without a Plan

You probably have already had challenging writing assignments that required you to research, then plan and write an informative essay. Whether the subject is a science, history, or another nonfiction topic, you need to decide in advance how you will organize your information and present it effectively. Don't just start *somewhere* and keep on writing until you have met the page requirement.

When you write an informative essay, the parts should *relate* to each other in a clear way to support your topic. A framework for writing can help you focus and manage information and ideas.

Framework for an Informative Essay
Introduction
Hook your reader's interest and clearly identify your subject. Make your topic and main point clear.
Body
Discuss each main idea in one or more paragraphs and support each main idea with facts, examples, and quotations.
Conclusion
Bring your essay to a close by tying your ideas together. Summarize or restate your main idea(s) or draw conclusions.

Developing Your Topic

When you develop ideas in the body of your essay, you may want to use a text structure such as comparison and contrast to organize information. If you use comparison and contrast, you can follow two different types of organization:

1. Point-by-Point If you follow this structure, the body of your essay will have a paragraph comparing or contrasting the student body of small colleges and large universities, followed by paragraphs comparing and contrasting the other two topics.

Topic	Small College	Large University
1. Student Body		→
2. Class Size		→
3. Organizations		→

Discuss the first point of comparison or contrast for both small colleges and large universities, then move on to the second point.

2. Subject-by-Subject If you use this organizational structure, your essay will have one or two paragraphs discussing the student body, class size, and organizations within small colleges, followed by one or two paragraphs discussing those same three topics as they relate to large universities. Discuss all the points about small colleges before moving on to large universities.

Topic	Student Body	Class Size	Organizations
1. Small College			→
2. Large University			→

You may also want to use **narrative description** to develop aspects of your topic. Narrative description is about real people, events, or procedures. You can use narrative description to provide an account of historical events or to add detail to a scientific procedure. General descriptions won't help your reader see your subject. Use concrete sensory details expressed with precise and vivid nouns, verbs, and modifiers. Use the following structures to organize your descriptions.

Organizing Description	
Chronological Order	**Order of Importance**
Describe details in the order in which they occur, especially in descriptions of events.	Start with the most important detail and work toward the least important, or vice versa.

Discuss and Decide

What descriptive details would likely be included in the essay on colleges and universities?

Analyze Two Student Models for Step 1

Luis used comparison-contrast to develop the content of his essay. Read his essay closely. The red side notes are comments made by his teacher, Mr. Sullivan.

Luis's Model

Topic	Albatross	Cormorant
1. Habitat	Lives far out at sea.	Never ventures too far from land.
2. Behavior	Solitary.	Social.
3. Special Adaptations	Adapted for life on and over the sea.	Adapted to hunt underwater.

Luis Medina
Mr. Sullivan, English
December 3

Two Water Birds: The Albatross and the Cormorant

The intro sets up what you are comparing and contrasting.

The albatross and the cormorant are two birds that spend their time in, on, and over the water. While both are winged creatures, their physical makeups are different. Each bird is designed to be better suited for its environment and survival tasks.

"On the other hand" is a good phrase to indicate a contrast.

For example, albatrosses, with their huge wingspan (the biggest of any bird—up to eleven or twelve feet wide) are rarely seen on land. They spend most of their lives far out to sea, riding the air currents or, when there is not enough wind, sitting on the surface of the water. Cormorants, on the other hand, are coastal birds that never venture too far from land. Because their feathers are not waterproof, they need to get dry after spending time in the water diving for food. You will often see a group of cormorants sitting on a dock or rocky pier with their wings outstretched, drying out.

You back up your claims with valid reasons.

The albatross is for the most part a solitary creature. It only gets together with others during breeding season, on remote islands out at sea. The female lays one egg per year; after the chick learns to fly, it heads out to sea and doesn't return to land until it is ready to breed, five to ten years later. Cormorants are almost the opposite. They are very social—feeding, traveling, and roosting in groups. The chicks in a cormorant colony are also social; they spend the day together in a "crèche,"[1] returning to their own nests for food.

The albatross is adapted for life on and over the sea. Because it spends so much time far from land, it drinks seawater, using a special gland located above the eyes to lower the water's salt content. Thanks to several adaptations, an albatross can ride ocean air currents for hours without once flapping its wings. For example, special tubes in its nostrils measure airspeed; a locking mechanism in the shoulder means it doesn't need to use any muscles (or energy) to keep its wings extended.

Meanwhile, cormorants have evolved to be speedy and agile underwater hunters. The bones of most birds are hollow, but a cormorant's are solid so it can more easily dive down and stay submerged. Its short, muscular wings help it to "fly" underwater. It can adapt its focus for both above and underwater vision.

Bones are a good comparison point, especially because you compare more than just the albatross and cormorant here.

As the saying goes, "To each his own." Albatrosses and cormorants each have evolved the physical and behavioral traits they need to survive and succeed.

---

[1] **crèche:** a group of young animals gathered together in one place, where adult animals can care for and protect them

A cormorant takes advantage of a raft to scout for food.

Discuss and Decide

Did the structure of Luis's model follow the text structure described in the source material? Explain.

Jenna's essay on flying lizards organizes descriptive details in order of importance. Mr. Sullivan made his notes in red.

Jenna's Descriptive Details
1. Appearance
2. Structure of Wings
3. Function of Wings
4. Defense Mechanisms
5. Diet

Jenna O'Leary
Mr. Sullivan, English
December 5

Winged Lizards

Nice intro. You start with a good hook here.

What if I were to say that lizards could fly? Would you believe me? You should, because deep in the forests of South India and Southeast Asia there is a group of lizards with wings.

There are as many as forty species of draco lizard, often known as gliding lizards or flying dragon lizards. Most of the time, a draco lizard doesn't look too special: He's a mottled brown, scaly little fellow, about eight inches long including the tail, and well-camouflaged on a tree trunk.

But folded up at his sides is something flashy and unique—a set of "wings" that the lizard can open and close as needed. The wings are actually flaps of membrane stretched out between long, extended ribs, in the same way that the fabric of an umbrella is stretched between and supported by thin metal struts ("ribs"). The wings are different colors in males and females and in different species, but are often bright shades of yellow, red, or blue. Draco lizards also have a colored fold of skin underneath the chin known as a dewlap.

Mentioning a jump comparable for a human is a good detail.

Dracos don't actually fly, but they use their wings to glide impressive distances—up to thirty feet. (Thirty feet is about forty-five times their total body length. It's as if a human could leap almost the length of a football field.) While in flight, they use their long tails to steer. Being able to glide from tree to tree in the forest

1. Analyze   2. Practice   3. Perform

helps them find food, escape danger, and defend their territory. They also use their wings and dewlaps to attract mates, and impress or scare off enemies and competitors.

When not gliding from tree to tree, draco lizards spend their time eating tree ants and other small insects. The males establish and defend a territory of two or three trees; the territory will include several females. The lizards spend most of their lives up off the forest floor (it's dangerous down there), but the females bravely head to the ground to lay eggs.

As exotic as they are, you might imagine that draco lizards might be endangered. Luckily, that is not true. (Perhaps) they are thriving because of the (mistaken) belief that they are poisonous. This is an adaptation that has helped draco lizards. There's no better protection from ending up as someone's dinner than looking unappetizing!

Your hypothesis appears valid, but think about stronger evidence to support the belief that the lizards are poisonous.

Close Read

Why is a descriptive text structure appropriate in this essay? Did it convey the lizards effectively?

_____

_____

_____

_____

Terminology of Informative Texts

Read each term and explanation. Then look back and analyze each student
model. Find an example to complete the chart. Finally, make a claim about which
model was more successful in illustrating each term.

Term	Explanation	Example from Student Essays
topic	The **topic** is a word or phrase that tells what the essay is about.	
text structure	The **text structure** is the organizational pattern of an essay.	
focus	The **focus** is the controlling, or overarching, idea that states the main point the writer chooses to make.	
supporting evidence	The **supporting evidence** is relevant quotations and concrete details that support the focus.	
domain-specific vocabulary	**Domain-specific vocabulary** is content-specific words that are not generally used in conversation.	
text features	**Text features** are features that help organize the text, such as: headings, boldface type, italic type, bulleted or numbered lists, sidebars, and graphic aids, including charts, tables, timelines, illustrations, and photographs.	

Claim:_____

Support your claim by citing text evidence.

_____

_____

PRACTICE THE TASK

What adaptations allow deep-sea creatures to survive in extreme environments?

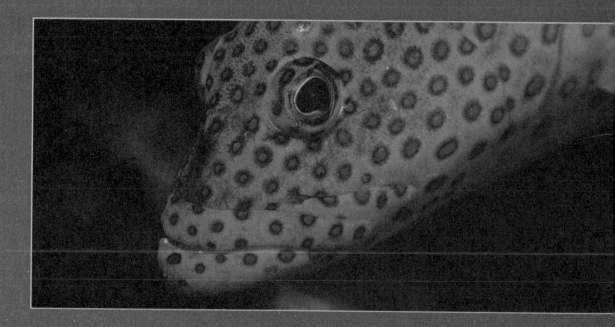

You will read:

▶ **A DATABASE**
Giant Squid (Architeuthis dux)

▶ **A SCIENCE ARTICLE**
Zombie Worms Drill Whale Bones with Acid

▶ **FIELD NOTES**
Trip into Blackness

▶ **AN INFORMATIONAL ARTICLE**
Deep-Sea Vents

You will write:

▶ **AN INFORMATIVE ESSAY**
What adaptations allow deep-sea creatures to survive in extreme environments?

Source Materials for Step 2

AS YOU READ You will be writing an informative essay about deep-sea creatures. Carefully study the sources in Step 2. Annotate by underlining and circling information that may be useful to you when you write your essay.

Source 1: Database

Giant Squid (*Architeuthis dux*)	
Anatomy	
Eyes	• Two eyes, each with a diameter of about 30 centimeters • Largest eyes of any animal on earth—great light-absorbing capacity
Funnel	• Located beneath the squid's body, or mantle • Pumps water, creating jet propulsion • Also serves to squirt ink, lay eggs, and expel waste
Feeding Tentacles	• Two tentacles, each up to 10 meters long • Tipped with hundreds of powerful, toothed suckers
Arms	• Eight arms, each about half the length of the feeding tentacles • Lined with thousands of powerful, toothed suckers • Guide squid's prey from its tentacles to its beak
Beak	• Located at the base of the feeding tentacles and arms • Slices prey into pieces for eating
Coloration	• At ocean surface: reddish orange to pink, with white mottling • In deep water: silvery to gold, depending on light source and angle
Ecology	
Range	• Worldwide • Rarely swims in polar or tropical seas—from distribution of specimens washed ashore
Habitat	• Probably prefers continental shelves and island slopes • 500 to 1,000 meters below ocean surface
Life Span	• Less than five years—as evidenced by growth rings in statoliths (mineralized organs that help the squid balance)
Reproduction	• Each individual probably mates only once
Diet	• Fish and other squids—from stomach contents of specimens washed ashore
Predators	• Sperm whales

Discuss and Decide

In what ways is the giant squid adapted for ocean living? Cite text evidence.

Zombie Worms Drill Whale Bones with **Acid**

by Martha Ennis, Zoological Manager

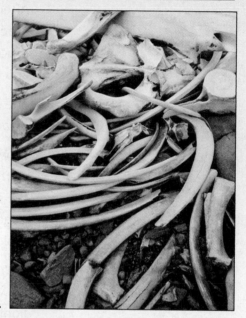

Monterey, California—A mystery of one of the deep ocean's strangest creatures, the "zombie worms" of the *Osedax* family, has been solved. Analyzing the worms' tissues, scientists have discovered enzymes that secrete acid. This acid is crucial to the worms' remarkable life history.

In 2002, scientists at the Monterey Bay Aquarium Research Institute accidentally discovered these small worms at the bottom of the sea off the coast of California. The worms live on the skeletons of whales, which drift down to the ocean floor and constitute a rich source of nutrients. Somehow the worms drill into the bones and extract the stored nutrients, but scientists were puzzled because the worms have no body parts for physically drilling into the hard material. Indeed, the worms lack even a mouth and gut.

Instead, it turns out, the worms have developed a chemical strategy. A zombie worm attaches to a whale bone with special root-like structures. The skin cells of these structures produce an acid, which dissolves the bone, allowing the worm to extract the nutrients.

This is just one of *Osedax* worms' unusual adaptations for life on the ocean floor. In a classic example of symbiosis, the worms depend on internal bacteria to digest the fats and oils extracted from their whale-bone diet. And only female "zombies" grow to adulthood. Males, which live out their lives in the gelatinous tubes inside each female, never develop past larvae.

Close Read

In what ways have zombie worms adapted to their environment? Cite evidence from the text.

_____

_____

Source 3: Field Notes

Trip into Blackness

by Arthur Jonssen, Marine Biologist
Mariana Trench, Pacific Ocean

11:20 A.M. The weather is good, and the sea is calm, so our dive can proceed. After climbing into the submersible, we test the motors, batteries, robotic arms, and CO_2 scrubber. We review safety and emergency procedures with the ship's crew. Finally, the hatch is cranked shut, and we are ready to go.

11:52 A.M. The submersible vibrates and tilts. I hear the squeal of the winch as we are lifted from the ship's deck and lowered into the ocean.

12:04 P.M. As we descend, leaving the world of sunlight behind, the ocean shifts from green to aquamarine to an intense glowing blue, like the sky just after sunset. At a depth of about 500 meters, the panorama outside our bubble darkens and our visibility reduces rapidly.

12:15 P.M. We're nearing the ocean floor at a depth of about 820 meters. The view outside is inky black. We keep the submersible's powerful lights off, for they might scare away our quarry. There! And there! We begin to see flashes of light—blue, yellow, red, and orange— as bioluminescent fish swim to avoid us.

12:48 P.M. A large jellyfish swims by, flashing bright blue lights in a circular pattern that also turns on and off. Here is a good example of a bioluminescent "burglar alarm." If threatened by a predator, the jellyfish's striking display might scare the predator away. Or it might attract an even bigger predator that could then eat the fish that was about to eat the jellyfish.

Close Read

Why does the jellyfish use bioluminescence as a defense, instead of remaining unseen in the darkness?

1. Analyze   2. Practice   3. Perform

DEEP-SEA VENTS

by Amy Bliss

Location Near Antarctica in the Southern Pacific, 7,200 feet below the surface lies a chain of hydrothermal vents. This area has only recently been explored by a team of scientists. Because scientists are not adapted for deep-sea life, they used a remote-controlled underwater vehicle to explore the landscape.

Climate It's very hot and very cold at the same time. Hydrothermal vents form where two continental plates collide. Cold seawater pours into the earth's crust and encounters molten rocks. Water spewing back out of the vents' chimneys might reach 700°F. A few feet away, water is barely above freezing.

This unusual geology creates an extraordinary biological opportunity. When frigid water meets hot rock, chemical reactions produce an array of mineral compounds, which many organisms consider food. Down here, the web of life depends on chemistry, not photosynthesis.

Yeti Crabs Gathered in heaps around the thermal vents, white crabs wave their claws together in unison. Dubbed "yeti crabs" for their hairy chests and legs, these creatures are new to science. And they are clearly thriving, with up to 600 "yetis" living on each square meter (about 11 square feet) of their favored real estate. What do they eat? Scientists aren't sure but conjecture that mineral-eating bacteria might grow on the crabs' hairs and that the crabs might scoop up the bacteria.

Discuss and Decide

How does the yeti crabs' diet work as an adaptation for their environment?

Respond to Questions on Step 2 Sources

The following questions will help you think about the sources you've read. Use your notes and refer to the sources as you answer the questions. Your answers to will help you write your essay.

1 According to the selections, which creature has an effective defense for scaring off a predator?

   a. the giant squid

   b. zombie worms

   c. deep-sea jellyfish

   d. yeti crabs

2 Which words best support your answer to question 1?

   a. "Tipped with hundreds of powerful, toothed suckers"

   b. "This acid is crucial to the worms' remarkable life history."

   c. "... it might attract an even bigger predator that could then eat the fish that was about to eat the jellyfish."

   d. "...mineral-eating bacteria might grow on the crabs' hairs, and that the crabs might scoop up the bacteria."

3 Which of these is *not* a characteristic of the giant squid?

   a. pumps water

   b. skin's cells produce acid

   c. toothed suckers

   d. a beak

4 What makes the yeti crabs best adapted to their environment, according to Source 4?

   a. their diet

   b. their hairy chests and legs

   c. their ability to move quickly

   d. their ability to live in a place where the temperature constantly changes

5 According to Source 4, how can you tell that the yeti crabs are "thriving"?

   a. Mineral-eating bacteria grow on their backs.

   b. They do not have to rely on photosynthesis to eat.

   c. They have hairy chests and legs.

   d. There are many yeti crabs alive on the vents' chimneys.

6 **Prose Constructed-Response** In "Trip into Blackness," what do you learn about being a scientist studying the deep sea?

_____

_____

_____

_____

_____

7 **Prose Constructed-Response** Would a giant squid be able to live comfortably alongside yeti crabs? Why or why not? Cite evidence from the selections in your response.

_____

_____

_____

_____

_____

Write an informative essay to answer this question:
What adaptations allow deep-sea creatures to survive in
extreme environments?

Planning and Prewriting

Before you start writing, review your sources and start to synthesize, or integrate,
the information they provide. Collect textual evidence in the chart below.

 You may prefer to do your planning on the computer.

Decide on Key Points

Summarize the main points and supporting evidence to include in your essay.

Characteristics	Zombie Worms	Giant Squid	Yeti Crabs
1. Habitat ☐ Alike ☑ Different	The ocean floor	Continental shelves and island slopes	Southern ocean in hydrothermal vents
2. Appearance ☐ Alike ☐ Different			
3. Diet ☐ Alike ☐ Different			
4. Predators ☐ Alike ☐ Different			
5. Age ☐ Alike ☐ Different			
6. Reproduction ☐ Alike ☐ Different			

Developing Your Topic

Before you write your essay, decide how to arrange your ideas. You can use one of the patterns of organizing described below or come up with you own arrangement—whatever works best for your subject and evidence. Begin your essay with an introductory paragraph and end with a concluding paragraph.

Point-by-Point Discuss the first point of comparison or contrast for both giant squids and yeti crabs, then move on to the second point. If you choose this organization, you will read across the rows of this chart.

Characteristic	Zombie Worms	Giant Squid	Yeti Crab	
1. Habitat				If you use this organizational structure, your essay will have a paragraph comparing or contrasting the habitats of giant squids yeti crabs, and zombie worms, followed by paragraphs comparing and contrasting the other points in your chart. Your evidence should include details that show how each creature adapts to its environment.
2. Appearance				
3. Diet				
4. Predators				
5. Age				
6. Reproduction				

Subject-by-Subject Discuss all the points about giant squids before moving on to yeti crabs. If you choose this method, you will be reading across the rows of this chart.

Topic	Habitat	Appearance	Diet	Predators	Age	Reproduction
1. Zombie Worms						
2. Giant Squid						
3. Yeti Crab						

If you use this organizational structure, your essay will start with one or two paragraphs about zombie worms, followed by one or two paragraphs containing points you choose to write about the giant squid.

As you write, look back at the selections for examples of descriptive details that you can use in your essay.

Finalize Your Plan

Use your responses and notes from previous pages to create a detailed plan for your essay.

▶ Hook your audience with an interesting detail, question, or quotation to introduce your topic.

▶ Follow a framework like the one shown here to organize your main ideas and supporting evidence.

▶ Include relevant facts, concrete details, and other textual evidence.

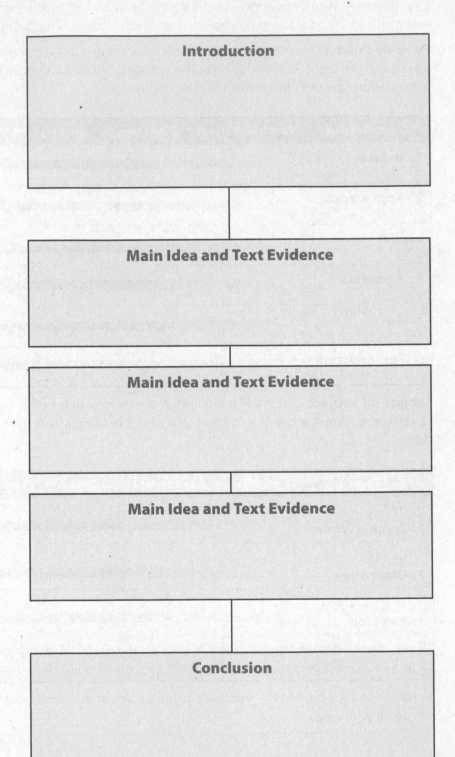

Introduction

Main Idea and Text Evidence

Main Idea and Text Evidence

Main Idea and Text Evidence

Conclusion

▶ Summarize or restate your main idea(s).

▶ Provide a concluding statement that ties together your ideas or reflects on the information you've presented.

Draft Your Essay

As you write, think about:

▶ **Audience:** Your teacher

▶ **Purpose:** Demonstrate your understanding of the specific requirements of an informative essay.

▶ **Style:** Use a formal and objective tone.

▶ **Transitions:** Use words and phrases such as *for example* or *because* to create cohesion, or flow.

Revise

Revision Checklist: Self Evaluation

Use the checklist below to guide your analysis.

 If you drafted your essay on the computer, you may wish to print it out so that you can more easily evaluate it.

Ask Yourself	Tips	Revision Strategies
1. Does the introduction grab the audience's attention?	Underline sentences in the introduction that engage readers.	Add an interesting question, fact, or observation to get the reader's attention.
2. Is each main idea supported by evidence, facts, and concrete details?	Circle evidence.	Add evidence if necessary.
3. Are appropriate and varied transitions used to explain ideas?	Place a checkmark next to each transitional word or phrase.	Add transitional words or phrases where needed to clarify the relationships between ideas.
4. Does the concluding section follow and sum up ideas? Does it give the audience something to think about?	Double underline the summary of key points in the concluding section. Underline the insight offered to readers.	Add an overarching view of key points or a final observation about the significance of the main idea and supporting details.

Revision Checklist: Peer Review

Exchange your essay with a classmate, or read it aloud to your partner. As you read and comment on your classmate's essay, focus on how clearly deep-sea creatures have been described. Help each other identify parts of the drafts that need strengthening, reworking, or even a completely new approach.

What To Look For	Notes for My Partner
1. Does the introduction grab the audience's attention?	
2. Is each main idea supported by evidence, facts, and concrete details?	
3. Are appropriate and varied transitions used to explain ideas?	
4. Does the concluding section follow and sum up ideas? Does it give the audience something to think about?	

Edit

 Edit your essay to correct spelling, grammar, and punctuation errors.

How have Australian animals
adapted to their environment?

You will read:

▶ **TWO INFORMATIVE ESSAYS**
Australian Fauna

New to Australia

You will write:

▶ **AN INFORMATIVE ESSAY**
*How have animals in Australia
adapted to their environment?*

Australian Fauna

by Deirdre Manning

AS YOU READ *Identify key terms and ideas to use in your essay. For example, "marsupial" is a likely term to be used in both sources.*

NOTES

Early in geological history, Australia was cut off from the rest of the world's land masses. This allowed a range of animals to establish successful populations in Australia—animals that were unable to do so in other parts of the world.

Almost all of Australia's native mammals are marsupials. Marsupials give birth to their young and then carry them in a pouch near their belly until the infant is old enough to survive on its own.

Another unusual type of mammal is the monotreme. Monotremes lay eggs instead of giving birth to live young. There are only two
10 types of monotreme in the world—the platypus and the echidna— and both of them are found in Australia.

Platypuses

Platypuses are found all along the eastern coast of Australia, from Tasmania to far north Queensland. They are small dark-brown furry mammals with webbed paws and a duck-like beak.

Platypuses live in burrows that they dig into the banks of rivers. They are diving animals, and can stay under water for up to two minutes. Unlike a duck's beak, the platypus' beak is rubbery and flexible. It has hundreds of electroreceptor cells inside it, which can detect the electrical currents that are caused by its prey swimming
20 through the water.

Platypuses give birth by laying eggs. The eggs are incubated by the mother in special nesting burrows. When it hatches, the baby platypus feeds on milk secreted from two patches of skin midway along the mother's belly.

Echidnas

Echidnas can be found all over Australia. They are small, round animals with large clawed feet, a long snout and a coat covered in sharp, flexible spines. Their diet consists almost exclusively of termites, which is why they are also known as spiny anteaters.

30 Echidnas also lay eggs. A single egg is laid in the female echidna's pouch and hatches in about ten days. The baby echidna (or puggle) lives in its mother's pouch until it begins to develop spines.

The echidna's spines are used mainly as a defense mechanism. When threatened, an echidna will either roll itself into a spiky ball or dig itself into the ground until only its spines are exposed.

Kangaroos

The kangaroo is Australia's largest marsupial. Kangaroos travel by hopping on their long hind legs, using their tail for balance. They can reach speeds of up to 56 kilometres per hour and can jump distances of eight metres and heights of almost two metres.

40 Kangaroos live in large packs (or mobs) of around 100. Their diet consists of grasses, leaves and other plants. They thrive wherever a regular water source is available. The introduction of European farming methods has established regular water supplies and allowed the kangaroo population to grow dramatically. It is estimated that there are around twenty million kangaroos in Australia.

A baby kangaroo is called a joey. Joeys are raised in their mother's pouch, suckling from the teats inside, until they are about ten months old. Within a few days of giving birth, female kangaroos enter into heat and will mate again and, if they successfully conceive, after one week's development the microscopic embryo enters a 50 dormant state that will last until the previous young leaves the

Discuss and Decide

How does the way platypuses, echidnas, and kangaroos give birth make them adapted for life in Australia? Cite textual evidence in your response.

pouch. The development of the second embryo then resumes and proceeds to birth after a gestation period of about 30 days.

Emus

The emu is a large, flightless bird with hairy, brown feathers. Standing up to six feet tall and weighing an average of 60 kilograms, it is the second largest bird in the world. Emus can be found all over Australia, away from settled areas.

Emus have a stride that measures around nine feet and can run at speeds of up to 50 kilometres per hour. They travel large distances in pairs or small groups, though occasionally large herds of up to a 60 thousand have been formed.

Emus have fairly large territories and can travel up to 900 kilometres in a nine-month period. If there is a reliable source of water, emus will stay nearby. They mainly tend to travel long distances in search of water. Their diet consists of leaves, grasses, fruits, native plants, and insects. Emu young are called chicks.

Wombats

The wombat is the world's largest burrowing herbivorous mammal. They average one meter in length and 25–35 centimeters in height. Wombats have four powerful legs that they use for digging, and large heads with small eyes, pointed ears and prominent snouts. Wombats 70 are found mainly on the east coast of Australia, from Tasmania to southern Queensland.

Wombats are nocturnal animals. Nocturnal animals are active by night and sleep during the day. During summer, wombats spend almost eighty per cent of their time underground in their long, complex burrows. They mainly leave their burrows at night when the air temperature is cooler, but in colder weather they can be seen out during the day as well.

Wombats are grazing animals, eating mainly grass and other plants, including shrubs, roots, bark and moss. When feeding, a wombat 80 can pick up its food with one of its front feet and place it straight into its mouth. Wombat young are called joeys and the female wombat has a pouch which faces backwards to prevent dirt from entering it when it is burrowing.

1. Analyze   2. Practice   3. Perform

Tasmanian devils

The Tasmanian devil is the world's largest carnivorous marsupial. It is roughly the size of a dog, and is thick-set with a muscular build, a large, wide head and a short, thick tail. The devil's fur is black and usually has patches of white on its chest and rump.

Tasmanian devils are only found in Tasmania, though fossil evidence shows that there were devils on the Australian mainland 3,500
90   years ago. They have powerful jaws and long, sharp teeth. They are primarily nocturnal, coming out at night to forage for food. Devils are scavengers, sometimes eating small mammals as prey, but mainly living on the remains of dead animals. When feeding, a Tasmanian devil will eat everything, including bones and fur.

Generally speaking Tasmanian devils are solitary animals, but packs of devils will feed communally on larger dead animals they find, like cattle and sheep.

Koalas

Koalas are tree-dwelling marsupials whose diet consists almost exclusively of the leaves of a particular type of tree called Eucalyptus.
100 Koalas have grey fur similar to sheep's wool, large prominent ears and a round face. Their limbs are long and muscular and their paws are broad with long claws. They can be found throughout mainland eastern Australia.

Koalas' paws have rough pads and long claws to help them climb. A koala's front paw has three fingers and two opposing digits, almost like two separate thumbs. The hind paws have a clawless opposing digit and two toes that are fused together to form a "grooming claw."

Koalas spend twenty hours a day sleeping or resting. The rest of the time is spent feeding, grooming and moving from tree to tree. The
110 koalas' diet of eucalyptus leaves is a very low-energy diet, which accounts for their low levels of activity. Their main source of water is the dew and rain that collects on the leaves they eat. Koala young are called joeys.

Discuss and Decide

How are Tasmanian devils different from the other animals listed in this selection? Provide at least two examples.

Source 2: Informative Essay

NEW TO AUSTRALIA

by Aidan Semmler

© Houghton Mifflin Harcourt Publishing Company • Image Credits: ©Image Source Pink/Alamy

AS YOU READ *Identify topics addressed in this article that were addressed in the previous source.*

NOTES

More than 80 percent of the plants, mammals, reptiles, and frogs found in Australia are not found anywhere else in the world. The only placental mammals (all mammals that are not marsupials or monotremes) native to Australia are the house mouse and some species of rats and bats. This is not to say that there are only these few species of placental mammals in Australia; rabbits, foxes, and even camels are common, but they were introduced species. Australia had developed an ecology that was unique due to its remoteness. Once settlers arrived, they brought with them familiar
10 animals, along with unexpected consequences.

The story of rabbits in Australia is a remarkable one. In 1859, a settler named Thomas Austin released 24 rabbits so that he could continue the hunting that he had enjoyed in England. Within ten years there were so many rabbits loose in Australia that even though about two million were shot or trapped each year, it didn't make a dent in their population. Over time, the rabbits have caused untold damage to Australia's native plants and animals. Destroying the plants has left less food for other animals and also causes erosion. The topsoil gets washed away and the land can no longer support
20 vegetation. Rabbits are thought to have caused more species loss in Australia than any other other cause.

Close Read

Explain what the author means by "introduced species." Cite textual evidence in your response.

_____

1. Analyze   2. Practice   3. Perform

Like rabbits, foxes were introduced in Australia for hunting. They were originally brought over in the mid-1800s. There are now more than seven million red foxes in Australia. They are a successful predator, responsible for the decline or extinction of many native species.

Other introduced mammals that cause damage include over a million feral camels, two million feral goats, twenty million feral pigs, and eighteen million feral cats. These animals have lived in
30 Australia for hundreds of years now, and have very few predators. This accounts for their huge successes as species, resulting in the major damage they inflict on the Australian ecosystem.

Perhaps most surprisingly dangerous to Australian ecology is a humble toad. The cane toad was introduced from Hawaii in 1935 to try to combat the native cane beetle, which was destroying much of the sugar cane crop. The cane toad population has now topped 200 million, causing major environmental damage. The toads are toxic, and native predators have no immunity to the poison. Toads can kill native predators such as the quoll, a cat-like marsupial that is also
40 hunted by the red fox. The cane toad does not seem to have had any effect on the cane beetle: The cane beetles moved too high on the cane stalks for the cane toads to reach.

Bearing in mind the havoc caused by species introduction, it is remarkable that people are suggesting the reintroduction on a large scale of another non-native species. The dingo is a wild dog that appears to have reached Australia about 4,000 years ago. It is believed that dingoes are descended from domesticated dogs and were brought by seafaring people from Asia. The dingo is now Australia's largest carnivorous mammal. (That position used to
50 belong to the Tasmanian tiger, a marsupial mammal that is now extinct. Tasmanian tigers were hunted enthusiastically in the nineteenth century, and the last of the species died in a zoo in 1936.) Most people regard the dingo as a true Australian because of its long residence down under. It is suggested that scarcity of dingoes allowed smaller, non-native, predators to hunt and cause the extinction of many native marsupials. Encouraging a larger population of dingoes to hunt these predators (and animals such as rabbits) might result in better conditions for native marsupials, which could flourish more easily than in an ecosystem in which introduced species either prey
60 on them or devour their food.

© Houghton Mifflin Harcourt Publishing Company

Respond to Questions on Step 3 Sources

The following questions will help you think about the sources you've read. Use your notes and refer to the sources as you answer the questions. Your answers to will help you write your essay.

1 Which of these animals might pose the greatest threat to Australia's ecosystem?

    a. Dingo

    b. Tasmanian devil

    c. kangaroo

    d. Fox

2 Which words best support your answer to Question 1?

    a. "packs of devils will feed communally on larger dead animals they find, like cattle and sheep."

    b. "There are now more than seven million red foxes in Australia."

    c. "The dingo is now Australia's largest carnivorous mammal."

    d. "It is estimated that there are around fifty million kangaroos in Australia."

3 Which of these is *not* a claim that you could make after reading the selections?

    a. Dingoes help keep animal populations in check.

    b. Australia has a variety of unusual animals.

    c. The young of many animals are called by a different name than the adult's.

    d. All of Australia's animals are introduced species.

4 **Prose Constructed-Response** Why is it advantageous for animals living in Australia to lay eggs or carry their young in a pouch? Use details from "Australian Fauna" and "New to Australia" in your response.

_____

_____

_____

_____

_____

Part 2: Write

ASSIGNMENT

You have read information about animals in Australia. Write an informative essay that examines how native and introduced species have adapted to life in Australia. Cite textual evidence from the sources you have read.

Plan

Use the graphic organizer to help you outline the structure of your informative essay.

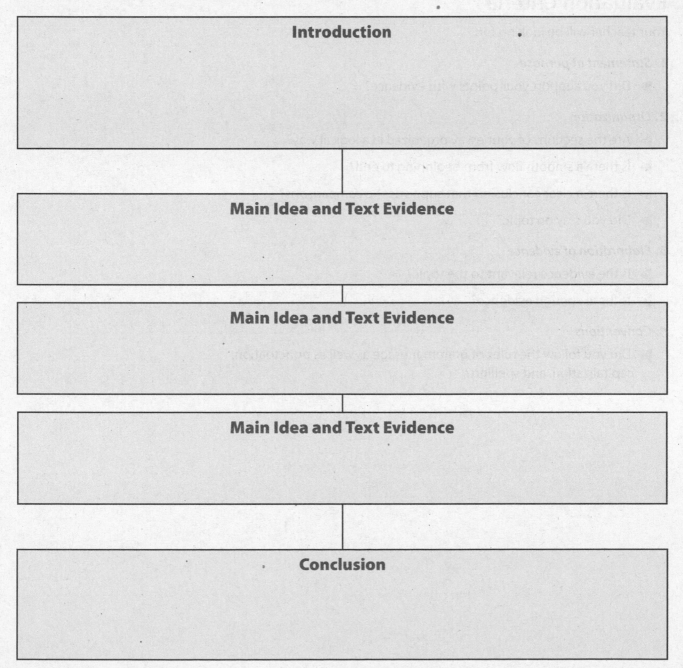

Introduction

Main Idea and Text Evidence

Main Idea and Text Evidence

Main Idea and Text Evidence

Conclusion

Draft

 Use your notes and completed graphic organizer to write a first draft of your essay.

Revise and Edit

 Look back over your essay and compare it to the Evaluation Criteria. Revise your essay and edit it to correct spelling, grammar, and punctuation errors.

Evaluation Criteria

Your teacher will be looking for:

1. *Statement of purpose*

▶ Did you support your points with evidence?

2. *Organization*

▶ Are the sections of your essay organized in a logical way?

▶ Is there a smooth flow from beginning to end?

▶ Is there a clear conclusion that supports the comparisons?

▶ Did you stay on topic?

3. *Elaboration of evidence*

▶ Is the evidence relevant to the topic?

▶ Is there enough evidence?

4. *Conventions*

▶ Did you follow the rules of grammar usage as well as punctuation, capitalization, and spelling?

Inspirations

Literary Analysis

STEP 1

ANALYZE THE MODEL

Evaluate a student model about author's craft and style in William Stafford's poem "Fifteen."

STEP 2

PRACTICE THE TASK

Write a literary analysis about Whitman's Civil War experiences as described in a poem and a letter to his mother.

STEP 3

PERFORM THE TASK

Write a literary analysis of the themes in "If—" and in "Kipling and I."

What inspires you? Which songs make your heart soar? Which stories make you believe that you can make a difference? The word *inspiration* comes from the Latin word *spirare*, meaning "to breathe," and has the same root as the word *spirit*. We humans need inspiration almost as much as we need air to breathe. Literature is a ready source of stories and poems that can lift our spirits, make us believe in ourselves, and help us survive and overcome hardship.

Literature allows us to see ordinary events in a different light. A teenager's encounter with a motorcycle in Stafford's poem "Fifteen" becomes a symbol for an adolescent yearning for freedom. "Kipling and I" by Jesús Colón tells the true story of a young man's struggles with poverty and the inspiration that helps him overcome his troubles.

A great believer in the power of words, the writer Walt Whitman celebrated the American spirit of individualism. He served as a nurse to soldiers who had fought in the bloody battles of the American Civil War. Whitman's life and work, featured in this unit, continue to inspire us today with their compassion, honesty, and unwavering belief in the strength of the human spirit.

IN THIS UNIT, you will analyze one student's response to the poem "Fifteen" by William Stafford. Then you will analyze how Whitman's experiences as a nurse in a Civil War hospital compare and contrast with his poem "The Artilleryman's Vision." Finally, you will analyze themes across cultures and genres in "If—" by Rudyard Kipling and in "Kipling and I" by Jesús Colón.

STEP
1
ANALYZE THE MODEL

What inspires us to grow and change?

You will read:

▶ **A BIOGRAPHY**
William Stafford: The Poet and His Craft

▶ **A POEM**
"Fifteen"

You will analyze:

▶ **A STUDENT MODEL**
Growing Up: Theme and Style in Stafford's "Fifteen"

Source Materials for Step 1

Mr. Lewis assigned the following biography and poem to his class to read and analyze. The notes in the side columns were written by Jennifer Ricardo, a student in Mr. Lewis's class.

William Stafford: The Poet and His Craft

Poet and pacifist William Stafford (1914–1993) was born in Hutchinson, Kansas. Stafford was the oldest of three children in a family with a great love for literature. During the Great Depression, his family moved from town to town seeking work. Stafford contributed to the family's income by delivering newspapers, working in sugar-beet fields, raising vegetables, and working as an electrician's apprentice.

A conscientious objector, Stafford worked in the civilian public service camps during World War II. His first major collection of poetry, *Traveling Through the Dark*, was published when he was forty-eight years old and won the National Book Award. He went on to publish more than sixty-five volumes of poetry and prose.

> *That's pretty late to start writing poetry!*

Like Robert Frost's poetry, Stafford's poems are deceptively simple—written in familiar language but focused on complex feelings and ideas. His subject matter is life in the western United States. In this locale, ordinary encounters reveal extraordinary moments. Stafford's poems are earthy and specific. The poet speaks in a gentle, slightly self-mocking, dreamy tone of voice.

> *Hmm . . . that should be interesting.*

> *I'd better pay attention to the voice in the poem.*

The people, animals, and varying landscapes were the backdrop of Stafford's life—and his writing. He wrote that the houses of his youth were always on the outside of town, on the cusp of "adventure fields forever, or rivers that wended off over the horizon, forever. And in the center of town was a library, another kind of edge out there forever, to explore."

Despite his late start as a poet, Stafford published six volumes of poetry, many prose articles, and a nonfiction book, *Down in My Heart* (1947), describing his experiences as a conscientious objector during World War II.

Fifteen

by William Stafford

South of the bridge on Seventeenth — alliteration
I found back of the willows one summer
day a motorcycle with engine running
as it lay on its side, ticking over

5   slowly in the high grass. I was fifteen.

I admired all that pulsing gleam, the
shiny flanks, the demure headlights
fringed where it lay; I led it gently
to the road and stood with that

10   companion, ready and friendly. I was fifteen.

We could find the end of a road, meet
the sky on out Seventeenth. I thought about
hills, and patting the handle got back a
confident opinion. On the bridge we indulged

15   a forward feeling, a tremble. I was fifteen.

Thinking, back farther in the grass I found
the owner, just coming to, where he had flipped
over the rail. He had blood on his hand, was pale—
I helped him walk to his machine. He ran his hand

20   over it, called me good man, roared away.

I stood there, fifteen.

"demure" usually describes a person, not a machine

motorcycle is like a horse—or a girl

Is the owner hurt? He calls the speaker "a good man" though he's only a teenager.

Discuss and Decide

What words in the last stanza signal a shift in the speaker's view? What does the speaker realize at this point?

Analyze a Student Model for Step 1

Read Jennifer's literary analysis closely. The red side notes are the comments that her teacher, Mr. Lewis, wrote.

Jennifer Ricardo
Mr. Lewis, English
April 24

Growing Up:
Theme and Style in Stafford's "Fifteen"

William Stafford's poem "Fifteen" is deceptively simple. One summer, a teenage boy finds a motorcycle and rides it. He then finds its owner, who has had an accident and has fallen, and the boy returns the bike to him.

Nice points about the "companion" motorcycle. I really like your idea about its being a symbol of love. Write some more about that!

There is much more happening in these lines than such a simple encounter, and the motorcycle is much more than an inanimate vehicle. The motorcycle is very nearly alive. It "pulses," and has "flanks," like a horse—or a large girl or woman. The narrator describes this adolescent fantasy machine, which has now become very close and near to him, as a "companion." "Trembling," he dares to go for a ride.

I like the points you make about theme. Can you unify them in an overarching controlling idea?

The speaker of the poem is fifteen, as he keeps repeating. He encounters this motorcycle as a young boy might encounter a girl or a woman, both attracted to her and terrified of her. This personification of the machine is a central part of the theme. The motorcycle, with all its glamour, could be a symbol of love.

The poet uses alliteration in this poem quite effectively. The *r* sounds in the poem help us hear the rumble of the motorcycle ("ready and friendly," "a forward feeling," "a tremble"). The *s* sounds convey the breath of the personified vehicle, and the heady season in the poem's key words ("South," "Seventeenth," "summer," "sky").

Freedom and temptation are the focus of the third stanza as the speaker imagines himself "stealing" the motorcycle and taking it for a ride. He clearly states that there is "a forward feeling, a tremble," a growing excitement rising within him. As he imagines finding "the end of a road," and meeting "the sky on out Seventeenth," he conjures up freedom and the thrill of the open road.

At the end, we discover the injured and dazed owner of the motorcycle. We see that the "friendly" creature, love, is not always so friendly and can throw one off balance and over the edge, literally and figuratively. The motorcycle owner is pale and shaken from his encounter, but ready to take the helm. He calls the speaker a "good man" and rides off, leaving the boy alone again, and "still fifteen."

Make your conclusion stronger by tying up your preceding points.

Jennifer, great job of interpreting the poem and its stylistic elements!

Discuss and Decide

Why does the author repeat the words "I was fifteen"? How does this repetition affect the theme of the poem?

Terminology of Literary Analysis

Read each term and explanation. Then look back at Jennifer Ricardo's literary analysis and find an example to complete the chart.

Term	Explanation	Example from Jennifer's Essay
main idea	The **main idea** is an observation or assertion about the poem or piece of literature.	
theme	The **theme** is the underlying message about life or human nature that the writer wants the reader to understand.	
tone	The **tone** is the attitude the writer takes toward a subject.	
figurative language	**Figurative language** is language that communicates meanings beyond the literal meanings of words.	
style	The **style** is the particular way in which a work of literature is written—not *what* is said but *how* it is said.	
voice	The **voice** is a writer's unique use of language that allows a reader to "hear" a human personality in the writer's work.	

How can real events inspire poetry?

You will read:

▶ **A BIOGRAPHY**
Walt Whitman

▶ **A POEM**
"The Artilleryman's Vision"

▶ **A LETTER**
Letter to His Mother

You will write:

▶ **A LITERARY ANALYSIS**
Compare and contrast Whitman's depictions of Civil War experiences in "The Artilleryman's Vision" and in a letter to his mother.

Source Materials for Step 2

AS YOU READ You will be writing a literary analysis that compares and contrasts Whitman's depictions of Civil War experiences in his poem "The Artilleryman's Vision" and in his "Letter to His Mother." As you read about Whitman's life and work, underline and circle information that may be useful to you when you write your essay.

Source 1: Biography

Walt Whitman

by Mark Botha

One of nine children, Walt Whitman (1819–1892) grew up in Brooklyn, New York, and Long Island and experienced both the community of country life and the urban bustle of a growing new city. As a young man, he plied many trades, including printer, teacher, and journalist. By the time he was twenty, his fascination with the boomtown atmosphere of Brooklyn led him to journalism. After ten years of reporting, he took a kind of working vacation—a difficult overland journey to New Orleans. He put his journalistic talent to work at the New Orleans *Crescent* while also observing the alien culture of New Orleans and the brutal face of slavery that existed there.

Returning to Brooklyn, Whitman served as editor of the *Brooklyn Freeman* while supplementing his income as a part-time carpenter and contractor. All this while, he was keeping notebooks and quietly putting together the sprawling collection of poems that would transform his life and change the course of American literature.

In 1855, Whitman self-published his groundbreaking collection of poetry, *Leaves of Grass*. Its original style drew lifelong admirers, including Ralph Waldo Emerson, and many critics, who condemned it as "disreputable." *Leaves of Grass* was expanded and revised through many editions until the ninth "deathbed" edition was published in 1892, thirty-seven years after its first appearance. It is a spiritual autobiography that tells the story of an enchanted observer who says how he is inspired at every opportunity.

When Whitman learned that his younger brother had been wounded in Fredericksburg, Virginia, he immediately traveled to the front. There he saw the aftermath of one of the war's bloodiest battles. This experience convinced him to work in Washington, D.C. as a volunteer nurse. While caring for the wounded, Whitman witnessed the effects of war on men's bodies and minds. During this time, he wrote numerous poems, including "The Artilleryman's Vision." His years of nursing, he once wrote, were "the greatest privilege and satisfaction . . . and, of course, the most profound lesson of my life."

Beset by ill-health, Whitman suffered a stroke in 1873. However, his influence continued to grow as he released new editions of *Leaves of Grass*. In the preface to one of these editions, Whitman wrote: "The proof of a poet is that his country absorbs him as affectionately as he has absorbed it." He believed there was a vital relationship between the poet and society. Whitman died on March 26, 1892. His funeral drew thousands of mourners, and his casket could not even be seen for the many wreaths of flowers left upon it.

Discuss and Decide

Why might Whitman have called his experiences nursing in the Civil War "the most profound lesson" of his life? What do you think he learned?

© Houghton Mifflin Harcourt Publishing Company

Source 2: Poem

Background: *Walt Whitman's "The Artilleryman's Vision" describes the nighttime dreams of a Civil War veteran after the war has ended.*

The Artilleryman's Vision
by Walt Whitman

While my wife at my side lies slumbering, and the wars are over
    long,
And my head on the pillow rests at home, and the vacant midnight
    passes,
And through the stillness, through the dark, I hear, just hear, the
    breath of my infant,
There in the room as I wake from sleep this vision presses upon me;
5 The engagement opens there and then in fantasy unreal,
The skirmishers begin, they crawl cautiously ahead, I hear the
    irregular snap! snap!
I hear the sounds of the different missiles, the short *t-h-t! t-h-t!* of
    the rifle balls,
I see the shells exploding leaving small white clouds, I hear the great
    shells shrieking as they pass,
The grape like the hum and whirr of wind through the trees,
    (tumultuous now the contest rages,)
10 All the scenes at the batteries rise in detail before me again,
The crashing and smoking, the pride of the men in their pieces,
The chief-gunner ranges and sights his piece and selects a fuse of
    the right time,
After firing I see him lean aside and look eagerly off to note the
    effect;
Elsewhere I hear the cry of a regiment charging, (the young colonel
    leads himself this time with brandish'd sword,)
15 I see the gaps cut by the enemy's volleys, (quickly fill'd up, no
    delay,)
I breathe the suffocating smoke, then the flat clouds hover low
    concealing all;
Now a strange lull for a few seconds, not a shot fired on either side,
Then resumed the chaos louder than ever, with eager calls and
    orders of officers,

While from some distant part of the field the wind wafts to my ears
    a shout of applause, (some special success,)
20 And ever the sound of the cannon far or near, (rousing even in
    dreams a devilish exultation and all the old mad joy in the
    depths of my soul,)

And ever the hastening of infantry shifting positions, batteries,
    cavalry, moving hither and thither,
(The falling, dying, I heed not, the wounded dripping and red I heed
    not, some to the rear are hobbling,)
Grime, heat, rush, aide-de-camps galloping by or on a full run,
With the patter of small arms, the warning *s-s-t* of the rifles, (these
    in my vision I hear or see,)
25 And bombs bursting in air, and at night the vari-color'd rockets.

Discuss and Decide

What is happening in "The Artilleryman's Vision"? What events occur in the present and which events occur in the past?

Source 3: Letter

Background: *In this letter to his mother, Whitman describes a meaningful encounter with a wounded Union soldier following the Battle of Fredericksburg.*

Letter to His Mother

by Walt Whitman

January 29, 1865

Dear Mother—

Here is a case of a soldier I found among the crowded cots in the Patent hospital—(they have removed most of the men of late and broken up that hospital). He likes to have some one to talk to, and we will listen to him. He got badly wounded in the leg and side at Fredericksburg that eventful Saturday, 13th December. He lay the succeeding two days and nights helpless on the field, between the city and those grim batteries, for his company and his regiment had been compelled to leave him to his fate. To make matters worse, he lay with his head slightly down hill, and could not help himself.
10 At the end of some fifty hours he was brought off, with other wounded, under a flag of truce.

We ask him how the Rebels treated him during those two days and nights within reach of them—whether they came to him—whether they abused him? He answers that several of the Rebels, soldiers and others, came to him, at one time and another. A couple of them, who were together, spoke roughly and sarcastically, but did no act. One middle-aged man, however, who seemed to be moving around the field among the dead and wounded for benevolent

1. Analyze   2. Practice   3. Perform

purposes, came to him in a way he will never forget. This man
20 treated our soldier kindly, bound up his wounds, cheered him,
gave him a couple of biscuits, gave him a drink and water, asked
him if he could eat some beef. This good Secesh, however, did not
change our soldier's position, for it might have caused the blood
to burst from the wounds where they were clotted and stagnated.
Our soldier is from Pennsylvania; has had a pretty severe time; the
wounds proved to be bad ones. But he retains a good heart, and is at
present on the gain. . . .

Walt

Close Read

Why might Whitman have been particularly interested in this soldier? Cite text
evidence in your response.

_____

_____

_____

_____

© Houghton Mifflin Harcourt Publishing Company

Respond to Questions on Step 2 Sources

These questions will help you analyze the sources you've read. Use your notes and refer to the sources in order to answer the questions. Your answers to these questions will help you write your essay.

1 Which of the following best summarizes the theme of Whitman's poem "The Artilleryman's Vision"?

   a. The true heroes of war are the officers and cavalry.

   b. War is a glorious pursuit that is worth all the pain and suffering it causes.

   c. War causes suffering and ends in death.

   d. War is hard on common soldiers even when the war is over.

2 Select the three pieces of evidence from the Whitman poem that best support your answer to Question 1.

   a. "While my wife at my side lies slumbering, and the wars are over long . . ." (line 1)

   b. "There in the room as I wake from sleep this vision presses upon me . . ." (line 4)

   c. ". . . I hear the irregular snap! snap!" (line 6)

   d. "The crashing and smoking, the pride of the men in their pieces . . ." (line 11)

   e. "The chief-gunner ranges and sights his piece and selects a fuse of the right time . . ." (line 12)

   f. "Elsewhere I hear the cry of a regiment charging, (the young colonel leads himself this time with brandish'd sword,) . . ." (line 14)

   g. "Now a strange lull for a few seconds , not a shot fired on either side," (line 17)

   h. ". . . (rousing even in dreams a devilish exultation and all the old mad joy in the depths of my soul,)" (line 20)

3 In what way does the historical context in which they were written affect the poem and the letter?

   a. Both works reflect the daily experiences of common Civil War soldiers in battle.

   b. Both works glorify the Union cause in the Civil War, which Whitman supported.

   c. Both works delve deeply into the feelings of the families of Civil War soldiers.

   d. Both works show that the common soldier in the Civil War was lost without his leaders.

4 Select the three pieces of evidence from the Whitman poem and the letter that best support your answer to Question 3.

a. "There in the room as I wake from sleep this vision presses upon me . . ." (poem, line 4)

b. " . . . tumultuous now the contest rages . . ." (poem, line 9)

c. "I breathe the suffocating smoke, then the flat clouds hover low concealing all . . ." (poem, line 16)

d. "He got badly wounded in the leg and side at Fredericksburg that eventful Saturday, 13th December." (letter, lines 4–5)

e. "We ask him how the Rebels treated him . . ." (letter, line 12)

f. " . . . good Secash, however, did not change our soldier's position . . ." (letter, lines 22–23)

g. "Our soldier is from Pennsylvania . . ." (letter, line 25)

h. "But he retains a good heart . . ." (letter, line 26)

5 **Prose Constructed-Response** How does Whitman's word choice in "The Artilleryman's Vision" and his use of phrases such as "rousing even in dreams a devilish exultation" (lines 20–21) describe his attitude toward war?

_____

_____

_____

6 **Prose Constructed-Response** How does the letter give you a glimpse into Whitman's sensitivity as a nurse?

_____

_____

_____

7 **Prose Constructed-Response** Does the poem or the letter offer a more disturbing view of the after-effects of war? Cite text evidence in your response.

_____

_____

_____

Write a literary analysis that compares and contrasts Whitman's depictions of Civil War experiences in his poem "The Artilleryman's Vision" and in his letter to his mother.

Planning and Prewriting

When you compare, you tell how two things are similar. When you contrast, you tell how they are different.

 You may prefer to do your planning on the computer.

Decide on Key Points

Summarize the key points that you will include in your essay. As you make notes about each point, identify how the themes in the poem and the letter are alike, and how they are different.

Point	Poem	Letter
1. Characters ☑ Alike ☐ Different	Civil War soldiers	Civil War soldiers
2. Theme ☐ Alike ☐ Different		
3. Genre ☐ Alike ☐ Different		
4. Speaker / author ☐ Alike ☐ Different		
5. Events (plot/story) ☐ Alike ☐ Different		

Developing Your Topic

Before you write your essay, decide how you want to organize it. For both organizational strategies, your essay will begin with an introductory paragraph and end with a concluding paragraph.

Point-by-Point Discuss the first point of comparison or contrast for both the poem and the letter. Then move on to the second point. If you choose this organization, you will read across the rows of this chart.

Topic	Poem	Letter	
1. Characters	→	→	If you use this organizational structure, your essay will have a paragraph comparing or contrasting the characters, followed by paragraphs comparing and contrasting the other topics in your chart.
2. Theme	→	→	
3. Genre	→	→	
4. Speaker / author	→	→	
5. Events (plot/story)	→	→	

Subject-by-Subject Discuss all the points about the poem before moving on to the letter. If you choose this method, you will be reading across the rows of this chart.

Selection	Characters	Theme	Genre	Speaker / author	Events (plot/story)
1. Poem					→
2. Letter					→
If you use this organizational structure, your essay will have one or two paragraphs addressing all your points as they relate to the poem, followed by one or two paragraphs addressing all your points as they relate to the letter.					

Finalize Your Plan

Use your responses and notes from previous pages to create a detailed plan for your essay.

► "Hook" your audience with an interesting detail, question, quotation, or anecdote.

► State your ideas about the themes in both texts.

► Chose the text structure: **Point-by-Point** Compare and contrast both subjects, one point at a time; or **Subject-by-Subject** Discuss all the points relating to the poem before moving on to the letter.

► Include relevant facts, concrete details, and other evidence. Restate your ideas.

► Summarize the key points and restate your main idea.

► Include an insight that follows from and supports your main idea.

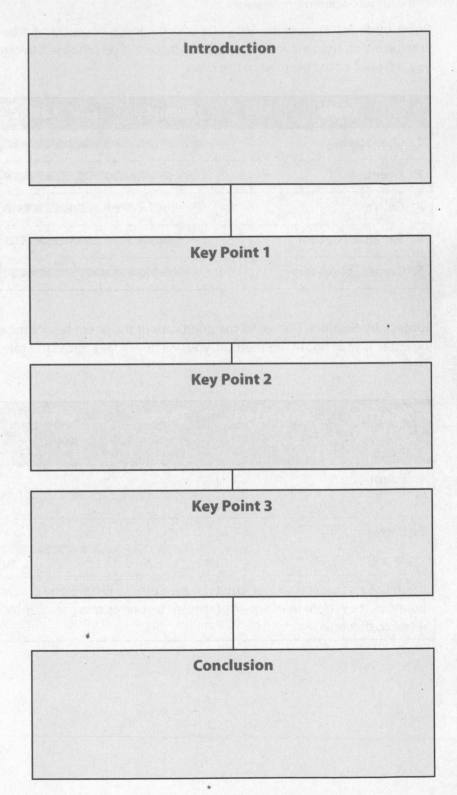

Introduction

Key Point 1

Key Point 2

Key Point 3

Conclusion

Draft Your Essay

As you write, think about:

▶ **Audience:** Your teacher

▶ **Purpose:** Demonstrate your understanding of the specific requirements of a literary analysis using a compare-and-contrast text structure with attention to theme and historical background.

▶ **Style:** Use a formal and objective tone.

▶ **Transitions:** Use words and phrases such as *both, and, like*, and *in the same way* to show similarities and words and phrases such as *but, however, while*, and *on the other hand* to show differences.

Revise

Revision Checklist: Self Evaluation

Use the checklist below to guide your analysis.

 If you drafted your essay on the computer, you may wish to print it out so that you can more easily evaluate it.

Ask Yourself	Tips	Revision Strategies
1. Does the introduction get the readers' attention and include a clear main idea?	Draw a line under the compelling introductory text. Circle the main idea.	Add a compelling introductory sentence or idea. Make your main idea clear and precise.
2. Are there examples of ways in which themes of the poem and the letter are alike, and ways in which they are different? Are the comparisons and contrasts supported by textual evidence?	Underline each example. Circle the evidence from the texts and draw a line to the comparison or contrast it supports.	Add examples or revise existing ones to make them more valid. Provide evidence from the text.
3. Are appropriate and varied transitions used to connect, compare, and contrast ideas?	Place a checkmark next to each transitional word or phrase. Add transitional words or phrases, where needed, to clarify the relationships between ideas.	Add words, phrases, or clauses to connect related ideas that lack transitions.
4. Is there a strong conclusion? Does it give the reader insight into the two texts and the themes ?	Put a plus sign beside the concluding statement. Star the text that supports the conclusion. Underline the insight that is offered to readers.	Add an overarching view of key points or a final observation about the two texts.

Revision Checklist: Peer Review

Exchange your essay with a classmate, or read it aloud to your partner. As you read and comment on your classmate's essay, focus on how the poem and the letter have been compared and contrasted. Help each other identify parts of the draft that need strengthening, reworking, or a new approach.

What To Look For	Notes for My Partner
1. Does the introduction grab the audience's attention and include a clear main idea?	
2. Are there examples that show ways in which the themes in the poem and the letter are alike, and ways in which they are different? Are the comparisons and contrasts supported by evidence from the texts?	
3. Are appropriate and varied transitions used to connect, compare, and contrast Ideas?	
4. Is there a strong conclusion that follows from or is supported by the preceding paragraphs? Does it give the reader something to think about?	

Edit

 Edit your essay to correct spelling, grammar, and punctuation errors.

PERFORM THE TASK

How can inspiration sustain us in difficult times?

You will read:

▶ **A POEM**
"If—"

▶ **A MEMOIR**
"Kipling and I"

You will write:

▶ **A LITERARY ANALYSIS**
Write a literary analysis that examines the universal themes in Kipling's poem "If—" and Colón's memoir "Kipling and I."

Part 1: Read Sources

Source 1: Poem

Background: *Rudyard Kipling (1865–1936) was one of the most popular writers in the world in the late 19th and early 20th centuries. "If—" is one of his best-known poems.*

If—
by Rudyard Kipling

AS YOU READ *Focus on the theme of the poem "If—" by Rudyard Kipling. Record comments or questions about the text in the side margins.*

NOTES

IF you can keep your head when all about you
    Are losing theirs and blaming it on you;
If you can trust yourself when all men doubt you,
    But make allowance for their doubting too:
5 If you can wait and not be tired by waiting,
    Or being lied about, don't deal in lies,
Or being hated don't give way to hating,
    And yet don't look too good, nor talk too wise;

If you can dream—and not make dreams your master;
10   If you can think—and not make thoughts your aim;
If you can meet with Triumph and Disaster
    And treat those two impostors just the same:
If you can bear to hear the truth you've spoken
    Twisted by knaves to make a trap for fools,
15 Or watch the things you gave your life to, broken,
    And stoop and build 'em up with worn-out tools;

If you can make one heap or all your winnings
    And risk it on one turn of pitch-and-toss,
And lose, and start again at your beginnings
20   And never breathe a word about your loss:
If you can force your heart and nerve and sinew
    To serve your turn long after they are gone,
And so hold on when there is nothing in you
    Except the Will which says to them: 'Hold on!'

25 If you can talk with crowds and keep your virtue,
    Or walk with Kings—nor lose the common touch,
If neither foes nor loving friends can hurt you,
    If all men count with you, but none too much:
If you can fill the unforgiving minute
30   With sixty seconds' worth of distance run,
Yours is the Earth and everything that's in it,
    And—which is more—you'll be a Man, my son!

Close Read

In your own words, state the theme of this poem.

_____

_____

_____

_____

Source 2: Memoir

Background: *Jesús Colón (1901–1974) grew up in Puerto Rico. At sixteen, he left Puerto Rico as a stowaway and ended up in Brooklyn, New York where his initial experiences provided the basis for this essay.*

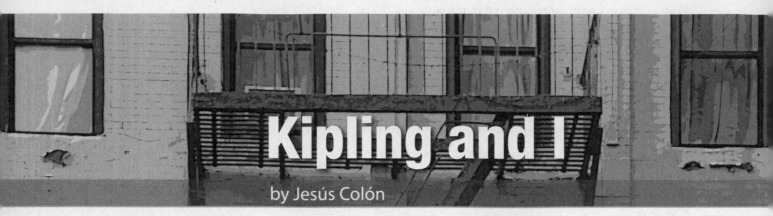

Kipling and I

by Jesús Colón

AS YOU READ *Think about the central message or idea that Colón conveys in this memoir. Record comments or questions about the text in the side margins.*

NOTES

SOMETIMES I pass Debevoise Place at the comer of Willoughby Street . . . I look at the old wooden house, gray and ancient, the house where I used to live some forty years ago . . .

My room was on the second floor at the corner. On hot summer nights I would sit at the window reading by the electric light from the street lamp which was almost at a level with the windowsill.

It was nice to come home late during the winter, look for some scrap of old newspaper, some bits of wood and a few chunks of coal, and start a sparkling fire in the chunky fourlegged coal stove. 10 I would be rewarded with an intimate warmth as little by little the pigmy stove became alive puffing out its sides, hot and red, like the crimson cheeks of a Santa Claus.

My few books were in a soap box nailed to the wall. But my most prized possession in those days was a poem I had bought in a five-and-ten-cent store on Fulton Street. (I wonder what has become of these poems, maxims and sayings of wise men that they used to sell at the five-and-ten-cent stores?) The poem was printed on gold paper and mounted in a gilded frame ready to be hung in a conspicuous place in the house. I bought one of those fancy silken picture cords 20 finishing in a rosette to match the color of the frame.

I was seventeen. This poem to me then seemed to summarize, in one poetical nutshell, the wisdom of all the sages that ever lived. It was what I was looking for, something to guide myself by, a way of life, a compendium of the wise, the true and the beautiful. All I had to do was to live according to the counsel of the poem and follow its

1. Analyze   2. Practice   3. Perform

instructions and I would be a perfect man—the useful, the good, the true human being. I was very happy that day, forty years ago.

The poem had to have the most prominent place in the room. Where could I hang it? I decided that the best place for the poem was
30 on the wall right by the entrance to the room. No one coming in and out would miss it. Perhaps someone would be interested enough to read it and drink the profound waters of its message . . .

Every morning as I prepared to leave, I stood in front of the poem and read it over and over again, sometimes half a dozen times. I let the sonorous music of the verse carry me away. I brought with me a handwritten copy as I stepped out every morning looking for work, repeating verses and stanzas from memory until the whole poem came to be part of me. Other days my lips kept repeating a single verse of the poem at intervals throughout the day.

40 In the subways I loved to compete with the shrill noises of the many wheels below by chanting the lines of the poem. People stared at me moving my lips as though I were in a trance. I looked back with pity. They were not so fortunate as I who had as a guide to direct my life a great poem to make me wise, useful and happy.

And I chanted:

If you can keep your head when all about you
    Are losing theirs and blaming it on you . . .

If you can wait and not be tired by waiting,
    Or being lied about, don't deal in lies,
50 *Or being hated don't give way to hating . . .*

If you can make one heap of all your winnings;
    And risk it on one turn of pitch-and-toss,
And lose, and start again at your beginnings . . .

"If—," by Kipling, was the poem. At seventeen, my evening prayer and my first morning thought. I repeated it every day with the resolution to live up to the very last line of that poem.

Discuss and Decide

Reread the excerpt from the poem. Why do you think it means so much to the narrator?

I would visit the government employment office on Jay Street. The conversations among the Puerto Ricans on the large wooden benches in the employment office were always on the same subject.

60 How to find a decent place to live. How they would not rent to Negroes or Puerto Ricans. How Negroes and Puerto Ricans were given the pink slips first at work.

From the employment office I would call door to door at the piers, factories and storage houses in the streets under the Brooklyn and Manhattan bridges. "Sorry, nothing today." It seemed to me that "today" was a continuation and combination of all the yesterdays, todays and tomorrows.

From the factories I would go to the restaurants, looking for a job as a porter or dishwasher. At least I would eat and be warm in a

70 kitchen.

"Sorry" . . . "Sorry" . . .

Sometimes I was hired at ten dollars a week, ten hours a day including Sundays and holidays. One day off during the week. My work was that of three men: dishwasher, porter, busboy. And to clear the sidewalk of snow and slush "when you have nothing else to do." I was to be appropriately humble and grateful not only to the owner but to everybody else in the place.

If I rebelled at insults or at a pointed innuendo or just the inhuman amount of work, I was unceremoniously thrown out and

80 told to come "next week for your pay." "Next week" meant weeks of calling for the paltry dollars owed me. The owners relished this "next week."

I clung to my poem as to a faith. Like a potent amulet, my precious poem was clenched in the fist of my right hand inside my secondhand overcoat. Again and again I declaimed aloud a few precious lines when discouragement and disillusionment threatened to overwhelm me.

If you can force your heart and nerve and sinew
To serve your turn long after they are gone . . .

90 The weeks of unemployment and hard knocks turned into months. I continued to find two or three days of work here and there. And I continued to be thrown out when I rebelled at the ill treatment, overwork and insults. I kept pounding the streets looking for a place where they would treat me half decently, where my

1. Analyze   2. Practice   3. Perform

devotion to work and faith in Kipling's poem would be appreciated. I remember the worn-out shoes I bought in a second-hand store on Myrtle Avenue at the corner of Adams Street. The round holes in the soles that I tried to cover with pieces of carton were no match for the frigid knives of the unrelenting snow.

100   One night I returned late after a long day of looking for work. I was hungry. My room was dark and cold. I wanted to warm my numb body. I lit a match and began looking for some scraps of wood and a piece of paper to start a fire. I searched all over the floor. No wood, no paper. As I stood up, the glimmering flicker of the dying match was reflected in the glass surface of the framed poem. I unhooked the poem from the wall. I reflected for a minute, a minute that felt like an eternity. I took the frame apart, placing the square glass upon the small table. I tore the gold paper on which the poem was printed, threw its pieces inside the stove and, placing the small

110 bits of wood from the frame on top of the paper, I lit it, adding soft and hard coal as the fire began to gain strength and brightness.

     I watched how the lines of the poem withered into ashes inside the small stove.

Close Read

Why do you think the narrator burns the poem at the end of the story? What theme, or insight about life, is suggested by his final actions?

_____

_____

_____

_____

Respond to Questions on Step 3 Sources

These questions will help you analyze the texts you have read in this section.
Use your notes and refer to the sources in order to answer the questions. Your
answers to these questions will help you write your essay.

1 **Prose Constructed-Response** What are the values set forth in the poem "If—"
that the writer Jesús Colón responds to?

_____

_____

_____

_____

_____

2 **Prose Constructed-Response** How are the themes of the poem and the
memoir alike? Cite text evidence in your response.

_____

_____

_____

_____

_____

_____

3 **Prose Constructed-Response** How does the poem "If—" sustain Colón
through his difficult times? Cite text evidence in your response.

_____

_____

_____

_____

_____

Part 2: Write

Write a literary analysis that examines the universal themes in Kipling's poem "If—" and Colón's memoir "Kipling and I."

Plan

Use the graphic organizer to help you outline the structure of your literary analysis.

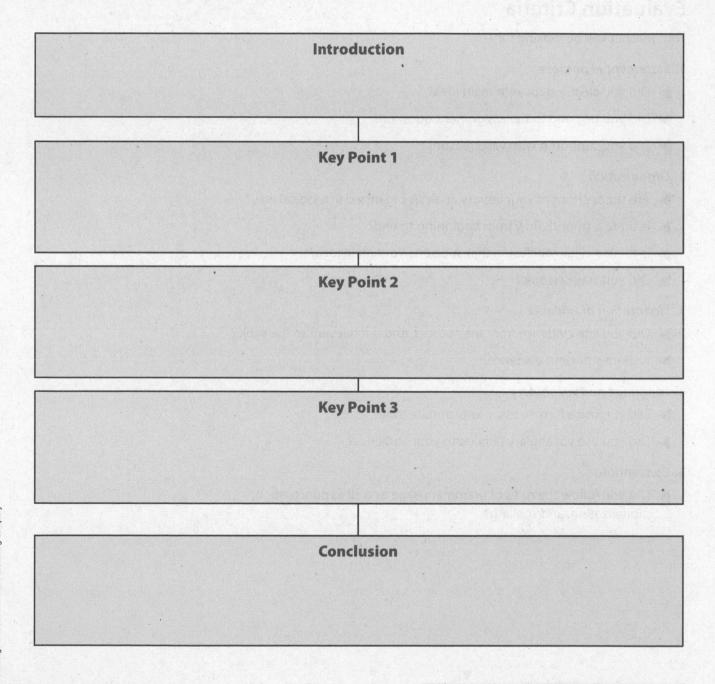

Introduction

Key Point 1

Key Point 2

Key Point 3

Conclusion

Draft

 Use your notes and completed graphic organizer to write a first draft of your literary analysis.

Revise and Edit

 Look back over your essay and compare it to the Evaluation Criteria. Revise your literary analysis and edit it to correct spelling, grammar, and punctuation errors.

Evaluation Criteria

Your teacher will be looking for:

1. *Statement of purpose*

▶ Did you clearly state your main idea?

▶ Did you respond to the assignment question?

▶ Did you support it with valid reasons?

2. *Organization*

▶ Are the sections of your literary analysis organized in a logical way?

▶ Is there a smooth flow from beginning to end?

▶ Is there a clear conclusion that supports your main idea?

▶ Did you stay on topic?

3. *Elaboration of evidence*

▶ Did you cite evidence from the sources, and is it relevant to the topic?

▶ Is there sufficient evidence?

4. *Language and vocabulary*

▶ Did you use a formal, essay-appropriate tone?

▶ Did you use vocabulary familiar to your audience?

5. *Conventions*

▶ Did you follow the rules of grammar usage as well as punctuation, capitalization, and spelling?

On Your Own

97

TASK 1

RESEARCH SIMULATION

Argumentative Essay

The mayor in your community has proposed new regulations involving restrictions on junk food, including soda, at area stores. A group of concerned students at your school will speak at the next city council meeting about the mayor's proposals. You have been chosen as one of the student representatives. To prepare for the city council meeting, you will write an argumentative essay explaining your position on the issue.

First you will review three sources concerning government regulation of food and drink. After you have reviewed these sources, you will answer some questions about them. You should first skim the sources and the questions and then go back and read them carefully.

In Part 2, you will write an argumentative essay about whether you agree or disagree that the government should be involved in this type of regulation.

Time Management: Argumentative Task

There are two parts to most formal writing tests. Both parts of the tests are timed, so it's important to use your limited time wisely.

Part 1: Read Sources and Answer Questions

Preview the Assignment

35 minutes

You will have 35 minutes to read three sources about government regulation of food and drink and decide whether you agree or disagree that the government should be involved in this type of regulation. You will also answer questions that will help you plan an essay on the topic.

35 minutes! That's not much time.

Preview the questions. This will help you know which information you'll need to find as you read.

How Many?

How many pages of reading?

How many multiple-choice questions?

How many prose constructed-response questions?

This is a lot to do in a short time.

How do you plan to use the 35 minutes?

Underline, circle, and take notes as you read. You probably won't have time to reread.

Estimated time to read:

Source #1: "Sugary Drinks over 16-Ounces Banned in New York City…"   ____ minutes

Source #2: "Food Politics"   ____ minutes

Source #3: "Should the Government Regulate What We Eat?"   ____ minutes

Estimated time to answer questions?   ____ minutes

Total   35   minutes

Any concerns?

_____

_____

Part 2: Write the Essay

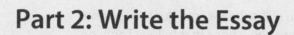

How much time do you have? Pay attention to the clock!

Plan and Write an Argumentative Essay

85 minutes

You will have 85 minutes to plan, write, revise, and edit your essay.

Your Plan

Before you start to write, decide on your precise claim. Then think about the evidence you will use to support your claim.

How do you plan to use the 85 minutes?

Be sure to leave enough time for this step.

Estimated time for planning the essay?	minutes
Estimated time for writing?	minutes
Estimated time for editing?	minutes
Estimated time for checking spelling, grammar, and punctuation?	minutes
Total	**85 minutes**

Notes:

_____

_____

_____

_____

Reread your essay, making sure that the points are clear. Check that there are no spelling or punctuation mistakes.

▶ Your Task

> You are doing research for a presentation at a city council meeting about regulations on junk food. In researching the topic, you have identified three sources you will use in planning an argumentative essay.

After you have reviewed the sources, you will answer some questions about them. Briefly skim the sources and the three questions that follow. Then, go back and read the sources carefully so you will have the information you will need to answer the questions. Take notes on the sources as you read. You may refer back to your notes at any time during Part 1 or Part 2 of the performance task.

▶ Part 1 (35 minutes)

You will now read the sources. After carefully reading the sources, use the rest of the time in Part 1 to answer the three questions about them. Though your answers to these questions will help you think about what you have read and plan your essay, they will also be scored as part of the test.

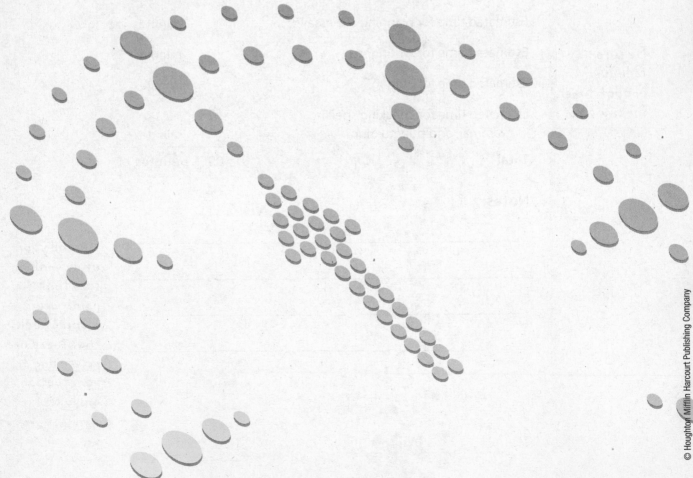

© Houghton Mifflin Harcourt Publishing Company

Sugary Drinks over 16-Ounces Banned in New York City, Board of Health Votes

by Ryan Jaslow, CBS News   *September 13, 2012*

Large sugary drinks are on their way out of New York City restaurants. New York City's Board of Health today passed a rule banning super-sized, sugary drinks at restaurants, concession stands and other eateries.

The ban passed Thursday will place a limit of 16-ounces on bottles and cups of sugar-containing sodas and other non-diet sweetened beverages beginning in March 2013.

The ban will apply in restaurants, fast-food chains, theaters, delis, office cafeterias and most other places that fall under the
10   Board of Health's regulation. People who buy sugary drinks at such establishments will still have an option to purchase an additional 16-ounce beverage.

Exempt from the ban are sugary drinks sold at supermarkets or most convenience stores and alcoholic and dairy-based beverages sold at New York City eateries.

City health officials called for the ban to combat the obesity epidemic. According to the NYC Department of Health and Mental Hygiene, more than half of adults are overweight or obese and nearly one in five kindergarten students are obese.

20   The restaurant and beverage industries have slammed the plan in ad campaigns and through public debates. The American Beverage Association has previously criticized that soda is being targeted as a culprit in the obesity epidemic over other factors.

"It's sad that the board wants to limit our choices," Liz Berman, business owner and chairwoman of New Yorkers for Beverage Choices, said in an emailed statement to CBSNews.com. "We are smart enough to make our own decisions about what to eat and drink."

Some medical professionals applauded the ban.

30   "For the past several years, I've seen the number of children and adults struggling with obesity skyrocket, putting them at early risk of

NOTES

diabetes, heart disease, and cancer," Dr. Steven Safyer, President and CEO of Montefiore Medical Center, said in an emailed statement to CBSNews.com. "This policy is a great step in the battle to turn this health crisis around."

Nutritionist Karen Congro, director of the Wellness for Life Program at the Brooklyn Hospital Center, told CBSNews.com, "There are pockets of the population who have no idea what a proper serving size is, so this will help reign them in." However she added 40 without educating New Yorkers about obesity risks, the ban may not be as effective as officials hope, given people will still be able to buy sugary drinks such as Big Gulps at 7-11 convenience stores.

"Unless they get the educational portion along with it, they won't understand why it's being a banned and how it relates to them personally," Congro said.

Some New Yorkers have ridiculed the rule as a gross government intrusion.

"This is not the end," Eliot Hoff, spokesman for New Yorkers for Beverage Choices, said in a statement to CBSNews.com. "We are 50 exploring legal options, and all other avenues available to us. We will continue to voice our opposition to this ban and fight for the right of New Yorkers to make their own choices."

SOURCE #2:

Food Politics

San Francisco Chronicle

In these columns from the San Francisco Chronicle, *Marion Nestle, a nutrition and public policy expert, answers readers' questions about food regulation.*

Soda-Size Cap Is a Public Health Issue

February 1, 2013

Q: You view New York City's cap on any soda larger than 16 ounces as good for public health. I don't care if sodas are bad for us. The question is "Whose choice is it?" And what role should the nanny state play in this issue?

A: As an advocate for public health, I think a soda cap makes sense. Sixteen ounces provides two full servings, about 50 grams of sugars, and 200 calories—10 percent of daily calories for someone who consumes 2,000 calories a day.

10 That's a generous amount. In the 1950s, Coca-Cola advertised this size as large enough to serve three people.

You may not care whether sodas are bad for health, but plenty of other people do. These include, among others, officials who must spend taxpayer dollars to care for the health of people with obesity-related chronic illnesses, employers dealing with a chronically ill workforce, the parents and teachers of overweight children, dentists who treat tooth decay, and a military desperate for recruits who can meet fitness standards.

Poor health is much more than an individual, personal problem. If you are ill, your illness has consequences for others.

20 That is where public health measures come in. The closest analogy is food fortification. You have to eat vitamins and iron with your bread and cereals whether you want to or not. You have to wear seat belts in a car and a helmet on a motorcycle. You can't drive much over the speed limit or under the influence. You can't smoke in public places.

Would you leave it up to individuals to do as they please in these instances regardless of the effects of their choices on themselves, other people and society? Haven't these "nanny state" measures, as you call them, made life healthier and safer for everyone?

NOTES

All the soda cap is designed to do is to make the default food choice the healthier choice. This isn't about denial of choice. If you want more than 16 ounces, no government official is stopping you from ordering as many of those sizes as you like.

What troubles me about the freedom-to-choose, nanny-state argument is that it deflects attention from the real issue: the ferocious efforts of the soda industry to protect sales of its products at any monetary or social cost.

Regulations Do Change Eating Behavior
August 31, 2012

Q: **I still don't get it. Why would a city government think that food regulations would promote health when any one of them is so easy to evade?**

A: Quick answer: because they work.

Regulations make it easier for people to eat healthfully without having to think about it. They make the default choice the healthy choice. Most people choose the default, no matter what it is. Telling people cigarettes cause cancer hardly ever got anyone to stop. But regulations did. Taxing cigarettes, banning advertising, setting age limits for purchases, and restricting smoking in airplanes, workplaces, bars and restaurants made it easier for smokers to stop. Economists say, obesity and its consequences cost our society $190 billion annually in health care and lost productivity, so health officials increasingly want to find equally effective strategies to discourage people from over-consuming sugary drinks and fast food.

Research backs up regulatory approaches. We know what makes us overeat: billions of dollars in advertising messages, food sold everywhere—in gas stations, vending machines, libraries and stores that sell clothing, books, office supplies, cosmetics and drugs – and huge portions of food at bargain prices.

Research also shows what sells food to kids: cartoons, celebrities, commercials on their favorite television programs, and toys in Happy Meals. This kind of marketing induces kids to want the products, pester their parents for them, and throw tantrums if parents say no. Marketing makes kids think they are supposed to eat advertised foods, and so undermines parental authority.

Public health officials look for ways to intervene, given their particular legislated mandates and authority. But much as they

might like to, they can't do much about marketing to children. Food and beverage companies invoke the First Amendment to protect their "right" to market junk foods to kids. They lobby Congress on this issue so effectively that they even managed to block the Federal Trade Commission's proposed nonbinding, voluntary nutrition standards for
70   marketing food to kids.

Short of marketing restrictions, city officials are trying other options. They pass laws to require menu labeling for fast food, ban trans fats, prohibit toys in fast-food kids' meals and restrict junk foods sold in schools. They propose taxes on sodas and caps on soda sizes.

Research demonstrating the value of regulatory approaches is now pouring in.

Studies of the effects of menu labeling show that not everyone pays attention, but those who do are more likely to reduce their calorie purchases. Menu labels certainly change my behavior. Do I really want
80   a 600-calorie breakfast muffin? Not today, thanks.

New York City's 2008 ban on use of hydrogenated oils containing trans fats means that New Yorkers get less trans fat with their fast food, even in low-income neighborhoods. Whether this reduction accounts for the recent decline in the city's rates of heart disease remains to be demonstrated, but getting rid of trans fats certainly hasn't hurt.

Canadian researchers report that kids are three times more likely to choose healthier meals if those meals come with a toy and the regular ones do not. When it comes to kids' food choices, the meal with the toy is invariably the default.

90   A recent study in *Pediatrics* compared obesity rates in kids living in states with and without restrictions on the kinds of foods sold in schools. Guess what—the kids living in states where schools don't sell junk food are not as overweight.

Circulation has just published an American Heart Association review of "evidence-based population approaches" to improving diets. It concludes that evidence supports the value of intense media campaigns, on-site educational programs in stores, subsidies for fruits and vegetables, taxes, school gardens, worksite wellness programs and restrictions on marketing to children.

100   The benefits of the approaches shown in these studies may appear small, but together they offer hope that current trends can be reversed.

Am I on Track?

Actual Time Spent Reading

SOURCE #3:
Should the Government Regulate What We Eat?

by Bert Glass

In December of 2006, New York City's Board of Health voted to become the nation's first city to ban the use of trans fats in restaurants. The new law, which officially went into effect in July of 2008, aims to eliminate the artery-clogging fat used in the preparation of many popular food items around the city, including pizza, French fries, and various baked goods. However, the ban raises several interesting questions in regard to the level of government involvement in regulating what we eat. When faced with the facts about the dangers of consuming foods prepared with trans fats, shouldn't it ultimately be each citizen's right to choose whether or not to consume foods prepared with the controversial item? Or is our government doing us a favor by making a universal decision to force us to find an alternative means of preparing food without the life-threatening ingredient?

Trans fats are formed when oils that are liquid at room temperature are mixed with hydrogen (a process called hydrogenation) and become solid fats. Many companies and restaurants choose to use trans fats in their food because they significantly increase the shelf life of their products. Also, trans fats are instrumental in creating a specific taste and texture in many foods that some consumers find desirable. Trans fats are also much easier to transport and ship than other oils and fats due to their unique solid state. However, all of these positives come with a dark side.

Advocates that support the ban on trans fats are quick to point out the negative health effects of consuming food prepared with the banned item. For example, trans fats can raise our level of "bad" cholesterol while also lowering our "good" cholesterol levels, both of which can contribute to heart disease. Also, the artery-clogging properties of trans fats can lead to a number of health problems requiring medical care, which can cost taxpayers billions of dollars each year.

The real issue at hand, however, revolves around the government's ability to regulate what we eat based on a number of unreliable health studies. Does this open the door to the government being able to regulate even the most minute details of our lives? For example, will the government soon be able to regulate what kinds of movies we're allowed to see in the theater, based on their arbitrary judgment of whether or not a film is dangerous to our mental health?
40 Will the government soon regulate our consumption of red meat, under the assumption that vegetables provide a much healthier alternative to the artery-clogging properties of a steak?

While it is easy enough to view the ban on trans fats as an isolated incident, such a ban ultimately puts the American values of freedom and individualism in jeopardy. If we no longer have the right to have a plate of French fries and a hamburger prepared with the ingredients we are used to, our American right to make informed decisions on our own without the government's intervention is in very big trouble.

Am I on Track?

Actual Time Spent Reading

Part 1 Questions

Answer the following questions. Your answers to these questions will be scored. You may refer to your reading notes, and you should cite text evidence in your responses. You will be able to refer to your answers as you write your essay in Part 2.

1 Using context clues, choose the best synonym for the word *advocates* in the following sentence in Source #3.

"Advocates that support the ban on trans fats are quick to point out the negative health effects of consuming food prepared with the banned item."

- **a.** opponents
- **b.** advancements
- **c.** journalists
- **d.** proponents

2 **Prose Constructed-Response** In Source #1, why did the city health department decide to ban sugary drinks over a certain size? What objection did some people have to the ban? Support your response with evidence from the text.

_____

_____

_____

_____

_____

3 **Prose Constructed-Response** Summarize Marion Nestle's two responses in Source #2. Your summary should be objective and free of bias. Be careful not to plagiarize.

_____

_____

_____

_____

► Part 2 (85 minutes)

You now have 85 minutes to review your notes and sources, and to plan, draft, edit, and revise your essay. While you may use your notes and refer to the sources, your essay must represent your original work. You may refer to your responses to Part 1 questions, but you cannot change those answers. Now read your assignment and the information about how your writing will be scored; then begin your work.

Your Assignment

It is time to start writing the argumentative essay on government regulation of junk food, which will serve as the basis of your presentation to the city council. Remember, your essay should explain whether you agree or disagree that the government should be involved in this type of regulation. When writing your essay, find ways to use information from the three sources to support your argument. A good argumentative essay should include a strong claim, and it should address opposing arguments.

Argumentative Essay Scoring

Your essay will be scored using the following:

1. **Organization/purpose:** How well did you express your claim, address opposing claims, and support your claim with logical ideas? How well did your ideas flow from beginning to end? How effective was your introduction and conclusion?

2. **Evidence/elaboration:** How well did you incorporate relevant information from the sources? Did you use specific titles or numbers in referring to the sources? How strong is the elaboration for your ideas? Did you clearly state your ideas in your own words in a way that is appropriate for your audience and purpose?

3. **Conventions:** How well did you follow the rules of grammar, punctuation, capitalization, and spelling?

Now begin work on your essay. Manage your time carefully so that you can:

- plan your essay, using your notes

- write your essay

- revise and edit your final draft

TASK 2

RESEARCH SIMULATION

Informative Essay

You are taking a world history class, and your teacher has assigned an essay about what makes a good leader.

First you will read three sources about leaders from different continents and different centuries. After you have reviewed these sources, you will answer some questions about them. You should first skim the sources and the questions and then go back and read them carefully.

In Part 2, you will write an informative essay about the characteristics of effective national leaders.

Time Management: Informative Task

There are two parts to most formal writing tests. Both parts of the tests are timed, so it's important to use your limited time wisely.

Part 1: Read Sources and Answer Questions

Preview the Assignment

35 minutes

35 minutes! That's not much time.

You will have 35 minutes to read three sources about historical leaders. You will also answer questions about the sources that will help you plan an essay on the topic.

Preview the questions. This will help you know which information you'll need to find as you read.

How Many?

How many pages of reading?

How many multiple-choice questions?

How many prose constructed-response questions?

Underline, circle, and take notes as you read. You probably won't have time to reread.

How do you plan to use the 35 minutes?

This is a lot to do in a short time.

Estimated time to read:

   Source #1: "Suleiman the Magnificent" _____ minutes

   Source #2: "Nelson Mandela Inaugurated President of South Africa" _____ minutes

   Source #3: "Accomplishments of Queen Elizabeth I" _____ minutes

Estimated time to answer questions? _____ minutes

Total   **35 minutes**

Any concerns?

_____

_____

_____

Part 2: Write the Essay

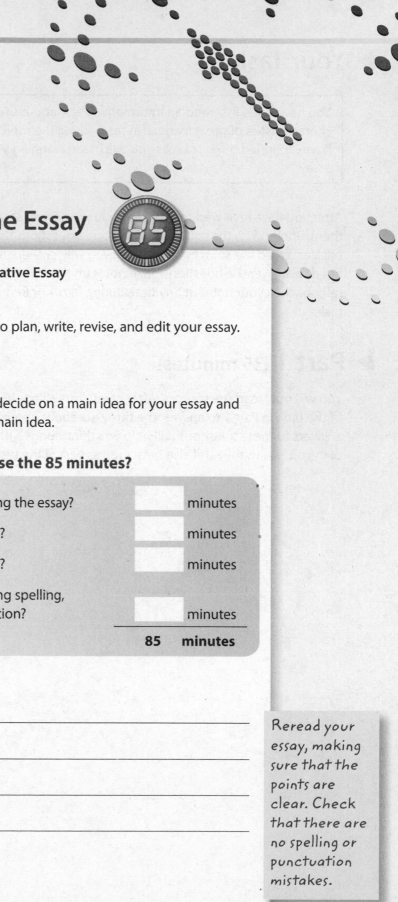

Plan and Write an Informative Essay

85 minutes

You will have 85 minutes to plan, write, revise, and edit your essay.

Your Plan

Before you start to write, decide on a main idea for your essay and details that support that main idea.

How do you plan to use the 85 minutes?

Estimated time for planning the essay?		minutes
Estimated time for writing?		minutes
Estimated time for editing?		minutes
Estimated time for checking spelling, grammar, and punctuation?		minutes
Total	**85**	**minutes**

Notes:

_____

_____

_____

_____

How much time do you have? Pay attention to the clock!

Be sure to leave enough time for this step.

Reread your essay, making sure that the points are clear. Check that there are no spelling or punctuation mistakes.

▶ Your Task

> You have been assigned an informative essay about the characteristics of great leaders. In researching the topic, you have identified three sources you will use in planning your essay.

After you have reviewed the sources, you will answer some questions about them. Briefly skim the sources and the three questions that follow. Then, go back and read the sources carefully so you will have the information you will need to answer the questions. Take notes on the sources as you read. You may refer back to your notes at any time during Part 1 or Part 2 of the performance task.

▶ Part 1 (35 minutes)

You will now read the sources. After carefully reading the sources, use the rest of the time in Part 1 to answer the three questions about them. Though your answers to these questions will help you think about what you have read and plan your essay, they will also be scored as part of the test.

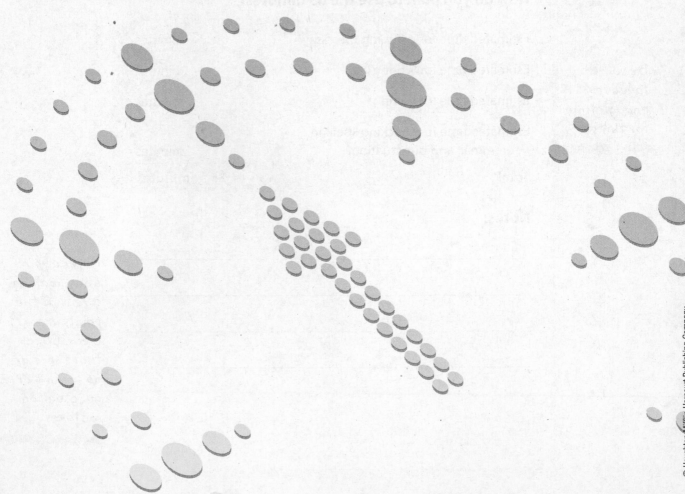

Suleiman the Magnificent

by Jane Simmons

In 1453, Ottoman armies from the western highlands of Turkey captured the city of Constantinople. They renamed the city Istanbul and made it the center of their growing empire. In 1520 a new sultan (supreme ruler) ascended the Ottoman throne. This sultan, Suleiman, became one of the greatest rulers in history. An aggressive military leader, he was feared but also admired by people in other lands. His people called him Kanuni, "the Lawgiver." Europeans called him Suleiman the Magnificent.

Suleiman the Warrior

The thunderous sound of goatskin drums and the clash of
10 brass cymbals reverberated off the great walls of the island city of Rhodes. This battle music was designed to strike fear in the hearts of its enemies. It had its intended effect. To the Greek soldiers on the ramparts, it seemed as if the very heavens had opened and let loose bolts of lightning and clashes of thunder. Even though it was extremely hot, the warriors felt a chill. After all, they were confronting the army of Suleiman the Magnificent, who had already captured the Eastern European city of Belgrade.

The drums and cymbals reached a crescendo. Suleiman's warriors raced forward to attack one of the most highly fortified
20 cities in Europe. In wave after wave they came, a hundred thousand strong. After more than 130 days of fighting, the Ottoman army entered Rhodes victorious.

Over many years, the fleets of Rhodes had intercepted Ottoman ships and disrupted its commerce. Now the routes were clear. After consolidating his victory and replenishing his army, Suleiman set his sights on other conquests. A soldier's soldier, Suleiman always rode at the head of his army to inspire his troops.

In 1526, Suleiman clashed with the Hungarian army. Leading the Hungarians into battle was their 15-year-old king, Louis II. The
30 fighting was over in a matter of hours, due to a brilliant tactical action by Suleiman. The Sultan allowed the charging Hungarians to

penetrate the front lines. Then he used an enveloping maneuver to surround them. Attacked from all sides, the Hungarians were wiped out, and their young king was killed.

Suleiman was not just a warrior. He was interested in learning, art, architecture, and the law. Under his reign the Ottoman Empire reached its peak both as a military power and as a center of culture.

Suileiman the Builder

On a hill overlooking the narrow body of water called the Bosporus stood Topkapi Palace. First built by Mehmet II, a sultan who ruled before Suleiman, Topkapi had been the chief residence of the Ottoman rulers since the 1460s. Each Sultan had added something to the palace complex, a tradition that was to continue for centuries after Suleiman's rule. Topkapi Palace wasn't just a home—its many chambers and outbuildings were a place where royal administrators met to run the affairs of state, soldiers trained, treasures were safely stored, and all kinds of artists lived and worked.

Ottoman architecture used elements such as domes, half-domes, arches, slim towers called minarets, and pillars. Buildings were often decorated with colorful tiles in geometric designs. Suleiman's chief architect was the brilliant Mimar Sinan whose works are still admired today. He and other architects built bridges, dams, fountains, palaces, and mosques throughout the Ottoman Empire.

Visitors to Turkey marveled at the way builders were able to complete structures so quickly, a rarity in Europe at that time. An Ottoman architect who designed a structure frequently lived to see his work finished. Historians attribute this quickness to the specialization of the workers. Ottoman records list workers such as wood sawyers to prepare the wood beams, carpenters to do the woodwork at the site, rough masons, skilled masons, quarrymen, plasterers, locksmiths, brick makers, and metalworkers. Like a modern-day assembly line, each kind of worker performed one task again and again. The benefit of this system was that everyone could work with speed and efficiency.

Suleiman, Poet and Patron of the Arts

In a courtyard surrounded by date palm trees, the poet Baki recited his poetry to an enthralled audience. Poets, artists, and philosophers used the courtyards at Topkapi Palace to present their works and exchange ideas. Suleiman himself was a prolific poet and writer.

70 Under Suleiman's rule, Istanbul became one of the world's cultural centers. Suleiman created many artists' societies that were administered from Topkapi Palace. These societies provided a training system for artists. The artists were paid fairly for the work they did. The best artists, including bookbinders, jewelers, and painters, were invited to become part of the royal court.

Suleiman's Legacy

Suleiman died in 1566. He left his successors a strong empire that was one of the world's most important powers. The efficient legal system, well-organized government, and strong military that he had built served the Ottoman Empire for many generations to come.

Am I on Track?

Actual Time Spent Reading

Nelson Mandela Inaugurated President of South Africa

by Matt Darvil

PRETORIA, May 10, 1994

NOTES

In a short but historic ceremony, Nelson Rolihlahla Mandela took the oath of office today as president of the Republic of South Africa. The ceremony took place at South Africa's main government building, in the nation's capital. Facing a crowd of 140,000, Mandela said that today's inauguration was "a common victory for justice, for peace, for human dignity." As the first black president of South Africa, the 75-year-old Mandela pledged to build "a complete, just, and lasting peace." He said, "The time for the healing of the wounds has come."

10 Vice President Al Gore led the official delegation from the United States. With him were his wife, Tipper, and First Lady Hillary Rodham Clinton. American civil rights leaders Coretta Scott King and Jesse Jackson were also part of the group. "The history we are present to witness marks a transition in the history of our world," Mr. Gore said.

Historic Election

Today's event is a result of South Africa's first "all-race" elections. In April, South Africans of every race were allowed to vote in a national election. Mandela, candidate of the African National Congress (ANC), won a landslide victory.

20 The path to the elections began more than four years ago, when President F. W. de Klerk persuaded white South Africans to work for change with black South Africans. A key part of de Klerk's plan was the release of Mandela from prison, where he had been for 27 years.

On the day of his release, Mandela spoke of the need for democratic elections: "Universal suffrage on a common voters' roll in a united, democratic, and nonracial South Africa is the only way to peace and racial harmony."

Mandela's Long Road to Freedom

Born in 1918, Nelson Mandela grew up in rural South Africa. White South Africans ruled the country, and black South Africans

30 suffered discrimination in all aspects of their lives. When Mandela was in his 30s, South Africa adopted an official policy of racial separation called *apartheid*. Mandela's battles against apartheid would put him in prison beginning in 1962.

Mandela used every opportunity he had to speak out against the injustice of white domination. "I have dedicated myself to the struggle of the African people," he declared during one of his trials. "I have cherished the ideal of a democratic and free society in which all persons live together in harmony and with equal opportunities. It is an ideal which I hope to live for and to achieve. But, if needs be, it
40 is an ideal for which I am prepared to die."

Mandela was held at the notorious Robben Island prison. Conditions were harsh—bare cells, meager food, manual labor, and scarce contact with the outside world. And yet Mandela never lost his spirit or determination. Other prisoners benefited from spending time with him, learning history and political strategy. Robben Island became known as "Mandela University."

Mandela was an international symbol of the injustice of apartheid. All over the world, people demanded, "Free Mandela!" The white leaders of South Africa began to offer him some form of
50 conditional release as early as 1985. But Mandela was not willing to accept conditions—or return to a country where he and his people still had no political rights. "Your freedom and mine cannot be separated," he told them.

When President de Klerk took office in 1989, negotiations began for South Africa's political future. Mandela was released in February 1990. The two men continued to work together to find a way to end apartheid. In 1993, they won the Nobel Peace Prize for their efforts.

Am I on Track?

Actual Time Spent Reading

Accomplishments of
Queen Elizabeth I

by Amit Carter

NOTES

Queen Elizabeth I has the reputation of being one of the greatest monarchs of England. The Elizabethan era is often referred to as the Golden Age of Britain. But what did "Good Queen Bess" do that made her so beloved of the English people? What were her greatest achievements?

The Major Accomplishments of Queen Elizabeth I

- She was a gifted scholar who was able to speak several languages including Latin, Greek, French, and Italian.

- During her reign there was a widespread increase in literacy and great achievements in the arts. Great poets and playwrights, such as William Shakespeare, Edmund Spenser, Christopher Marlowe, and Sir Walter Raleigh created works that are still greatly admired and enjoyed.

- She greatly expanded the British Empire. She financed the explorations of such great explorers as Sir Francis Drake, Sir Walter Raleigh, Sir John Hawkins, Sir Humphrey Gilbert, and Sir Richard Greenville.

- She encouraged new scientific thinking, and important men such as Sir Francis Bacon and Dr. John Dee emerged during the Elizabethan era.

- She was thought of as a good and wise ruler, who was truly loved by her people. Her early education helped make her highly accomplished in the art of rhetoric and public relations.

- She surrounded herself with highly intelligent, loyal advisors such as Sir William Cecil, Sir Francis Walsingham, and Sir Robert Cecil who gave her sound political advice.

- A small fleet of British navy ships, with the help of some armed merchant vessels, defeated a much larger Spanish Armada.

Am I on Track?

Actual Time Spent Reading

Part 1 Questions

Answer the following questions. You may refer to your reading notes, and you should cite text evidence in your responses. Your answers to these questions will be scored. You will be able to refer to your answers as you write your essay in Part 2.

1 List one achievement that demonstrates good leadership for each of the persons discussed in the three sources. Support your response with evidence from the sources, and be sure to cite each source by number or name.

_____

_____

_____

_____

_____

2 Which of the following claims is **best** supported by information from the sources?

a. Suleiman was a more successful warrior than builder.

b. Nelson Mandela had little effect on the movement against apartheid.

c. Elizabeth I valued the counsel of others.

d. Elizabeth I confined her reforms to Britain.

3 Which piece of evidence **best** supports your answer to Question 2?

a. "Under his reign the Ottoman Empire reached its peak both as a military power and as a center of culture." (Source #1, lines 36–37)

b. "Mandela was an international symbol of the injustice of apartheid." (Source #2, lines 47–48)

c. "... Sir Robert Cecil who gave her sound political advice ..." (Source #3, lines 24–25)

d. "She financed the explorations of such great explorers as Sir Francis Drake ..."(Source #3, lines 13–14)

▶ Part 2 (85 minutes)

You now have 85 minutes to review your notes and sources, and to plan, draft, revise, and edit your essay. While you may use your notes and refer to the texts, your essay must represent your original work. You may refer to your responses to Part 1 questions, but you cannot change the answers. Now read your assignment and the information about how your writing will be scored; then begin your work.

Your Assignment

It is time to start writing your informative essay about the characteristics of good leaders for your world history class. When writing your essay, find ways to use information from the three sources to support your thesis. Be sure to present your ideas in a logical order.

Informative Essay Scoring

Your essay will be scored using the following:

1. **Organization/purpose:** How well did you state your thesis and support your thesis with a logical progression of ideas? Did you use a variety of transitions between ideas? Was your focus narrow enough to lead to a well-formed conclusion?

2. **Evidence/elaboration:** How well did you incorporate relevant information from the sources? How well did you provide elaboration for your ideas? Did you use precise language appropriate to your audience and purpose?

3. **Conventions:** How well did you follow the rules of grammar, punctuation, capitalization, and spelling?

Now begin work on your essay. Manage your time carefully so that you can:

- plan your essay, using your notes

- write your essay

- revise and edit your final draft

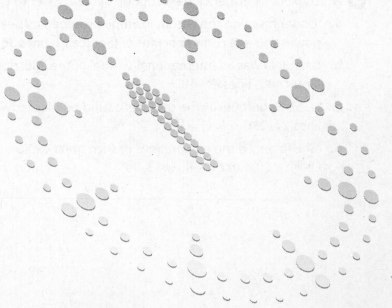

Time Management: Literary Analysis Task

TASK 3

Literary Analysis

As part of an essay contest, you have been asked to write a literary analysis of Edgar Allan Poe's classic poem "The Raven." You have identified two essays about Poe to use as part of your analysis.

First you will review the poem and the two other sources. After you have reviewed these sources, you will answer some questions about them. You should first skim the sources and the questions and then go back and read them carefully.

In Part 2, you will write a literary analysis of "The Raven."

Time Management: Literary Analysis Task

Most formal writing tests are made up of two parts. Both parts of the tests are timed, so it's important to use your limited time wisely.

Part 1: Read Sources and Answer Questions

Preview the Assignment

35 minutes

You will have 35 minutes to read two essays and the famous poem "The Raven" by Edgar Allan Poe. You will also answer questions about the sources that will help you plan your literary analysis.

35 minutes! That's not much time.

Preview the questions. This will help you know which information you'll need to find as you read.

How Many?

How many pages of reading?

How many multiple-choice questions?

How many prose constructed-response questions?

Underline, circle, and take notes as you read. You probably won't have time to reread.

How do you plan to use the 35 minutes?

This is a lot to do in a short time.

Estimated time to read:

Source #1: "Edgar Allan Poe"	minutes
Source #2: "The Raven"	minutes
Source #3: "Poe's Process: Writing 'The Raven'"	minutes
Estimated time to answer questions?	minutes
Total	**35** minutes

Any concerns?

_____

_____

_____

Part 2: Write the Analysis

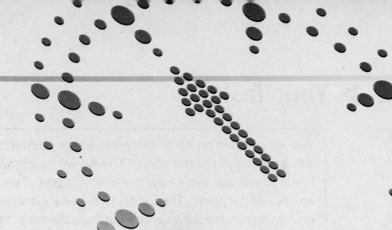

© Houghton Mifflin Harcourt Publishing Company

How much time do you have? Pay attention to the clock!

Plan and Write a Literary Analysis

85 minutes

You will have 85 minutes to plan, write, revise, and edit your literary analysis.

Your Plan

Before you start writing, decide how you will structure your literary analysis.

How do you plan to use the 85 minutes?

Estimated time for planning the essay?	minutes
Estimated time for writing?	minutes
Estimated time for editing?	minutes
Estimated time for checking spelling, grammar, punctuation?	minutes
Total	**85** minutes

Be sure to leave enough time for this step.

Notes:

_____

_____

_____

_____

Reread your essay, making sure that the points are clear. Check that there are no spelling or punctuation mistakes.

▶ Your Task

> You are entering an essay contest in which you must write a literary analysis of the poem "The Raven" by Edgar Allan Poe. You will use two essays about Poe as part of your analysis of the poem. The focus of your analysis should be on how the poem represents what Poe called the "human thirst for self-torture."

After you have reviewed the sources, you will answer some questions about them. Briefly skim the sources and the questions that follow. Then, go back and read the sources carefully so you will have the information you will need to answer the questions. Take notes on the sources as you read. You may refer back to your notes at any time during Part 1 or Part 2 of the performance task.

▶ Part 1 (35 minutes)

You will now read the sources. After carefully reading the sources, use the rest of the time in Part 1 to answer the questions about them. Though your answers to these questions will help you think about what you have read and plan your essay, they will also be scored as part of the test.

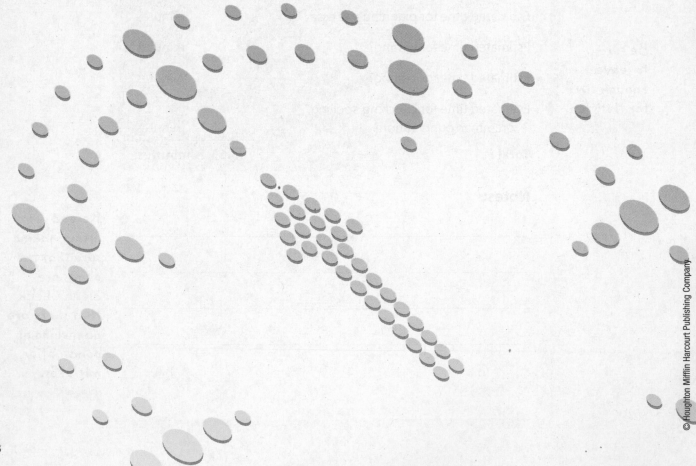

Edgar Allan Poe

by Lynn Malle

The author of "The Raven," which numbers among the best-known poems in American literature, Edgar Allan Poe (c. 1809–1849) was a master of the horror tale and the psychological thriller. His tales of the gruesome and grotesque contain distraught narrators, mentally deranged heroes, and doomed heroines. His stories and poems, steeped in Gothic horror, move beyond the rational world to explore the dark, irrational depths of the human mind. A poet, literary critic, and an innovator of fiction, Poe was once called one of literature's
10 "most brilliant, but erratic, stars."

Well known for his unstable life and for his formidable talent, Poe was abandoned by his father as an infant. Tragically, he lost his mother to tuberculosis when he was three and was taken in by John Allan, a wealthy Virginia businessman. However, Allan and he had a stormy relationship, and at age 18, Poe was forced to leave due to financial difficulty, thus beginning a lifelong pattern of self-destruction. Estranged from Allan as a young man, Poe formed a new family with his aunt and his young cousin, Virginia Clemm, whom he married
20 when she was only 13 or 14, probably marrying her secretly and then publicly a year later, in 1836. Unfortunately, Virginia died 11 years after their marriage, and Poe, who was devastated by her death, died two years later.

For much of his adult life, Poe struggled to support his family. He landed promising positions at several literary magazines, spoiling one opportunity after another with his erratic behavior. At the same time, his scathing reviews made him a feared and respected literary critic, and his inventive short stories brought him fame as a fiction writer. Although
30 his life matched the romantic ideal of the starving artist who suffered for the purity of his art, Poe's stories were designed to reach a large audience. His success with horror, science fiction, and detective stories proved his mastery of popular genres.

© Houghton Mifflin Harcourt Publishing Company

Poe's distinctive themes included madness, untimely death, and obsession. Given his troubled life, many critics have interpreted his deranged narrators, including the speaker in "The Raven," as reflections of the author's own tortured state of mind. However, Poe was a brilliant and controlled stylist, whose theories of art championed rigorous structure,

40 careful use of language, and the masterful creation of a single, calculated effect. In summary, Poe's fascination with the macabre, equaled by his interest in beauty and logic, exemplify the deeper divisions of the self and its shadowy side: the conflict of beautiful ideals with the darker impulses of human nature.

Am I on Track?

Actual Time Spent Reading

SOURCE #2:

The Raven

by Edgar Allan Poe

© Houghton Mifflin Harcourt Publishing Company

Once upon a midnight dreary, while I pondered, weak and weary,
Over many a quaint and curious volume of forgotten lore—
While I nodded, nearly napping, suddenly there came a tapping,
As of someone gently rapping, rapping at my chamber door—
5 "'Tis some visitor," I muttered, "tapping at my chamber door—
       Only this and nothing more."

Ah, distinctly I remember it was in the bleak December;
And each separate dying ember wrought its ghost upon the floor.
Eagerly I wished the morrow;—vainly I had sought to borrow
10 From my books surcease of sorrow—sorrow for the lost Lenore—
For the rare and radiant maiden whom the angels name Lenore—
       Nameless *here* for evermore.

And the silken, sad, uncertain rustling of each purple curtain
Thrilled me—filled me with fantastic terrors never felt before;
15 So that now, to still the beating of my heart, I stood repeating
"'Tis some visitor entreating entrance at my chamber door—
Some late visitor entreating entrance at my chamber door;—
       This it is and nothing more."

Presently my soul grew stronger; hesitating then no longer,
20 "Sir," said I, "or Madam, truly your forgiveness I implore;
 But the fact is I was napping, and so gently you came rapping,
And so faintly you came tapping, tapping at my chamber door,
That I scarce was sure I heard you"—here I opened wide the door;—
       Darkness there and nothing more.

25 Deep into that darkness peering, long I stood there wondering, fearing,
Doubting, dreaming dreams no mortal ever dared to dream before;
But the silence was unbroken, and the stillness gave no token,
And the only word there spoken was the whispered word, "Lenore?"
This I whispered, and an echo murmured back the word, "Lenore!"
30   Merely this and nothing more.

Back into the chamber turning, all my soul within me burning,
Soon again I heard a tapping somewhat louder than before.
"Surely," said I, "surely that is something at my window lattice;
Let me see, then, what thereat is, and this mystery explore—
35   Let my heart be still a moment and this mystery explore;—
        'Tis the wind and nothing more!"

Open here I flung the shutter, when, with many a flirt and flutter,
In there stepped a stately Raven of the saintly days of yore;
Not the least obeisance made he; not a minute stopped or stayed he;
40   But, with mien of lord or lady, perched above my chamber door—
   Perched upon a bust of Pallas° just above my chamber door—
        Perched, and sat, and nothing more.

Then this ebony bird beguiling my sad fancy into smiling,
By the grave and stern decorum of the countenance it wore,
45   "Though thy crest be shorn and shaven, thou," I said, "art sure no craven,
   Ghastly grim and ancient Raven wandering from the Nightly shore—
   Tell me what thy lordly name is on the Night's Plutonian shore!"
        Quoth the Raven "Nevermore."

Much I marveled this ungainly fowl to hear discourse so plainly,
50   Though its answer little meaning—little relevancy bore;
For we cannot help agreeing that no living human being
Ever yet was blessed with seeing bird above his chamber door—
Bird or beast upon the sculptured bust above his chamber door,
        With such name as "Nevermore."

55   But the Raven, sitting lonely on the placid bust, spoke only
That one word, as if his soul in that one word he did outpour.
Nothing farther then he uttered—not a feather then he fluttered—
Till I scarcely more than muttered "Other friends have flown before—
On the morrow *he* will leave me, as my Hopes have flown before."
60   Then the bird said "Nevermore."

---

41. Pallas: Pallas Athena, the Greek goddess of wisdom.

Startled at the stillness broken by reply so aptly spoken,

"Doubtless," said I, "what it utters is its only stock and store

Caught from some unhappy master whom unmerciful Disaster

Followed fast and followed faster till his songs one burden bore—

65 Till the dirges of his Hope that melancholy burden bore

        Of 'Never—nevermore.'"

But the Raven still beguiling my sad fancy into smiling,

Straight I wheeled a cushioned seat in front of bird, and bust and door;

Then, upon the velvet sinking, I betook myself to linking

70 Fancy unto fancy, thinking what this ominous bird of yore—

What this grim, ungainly, ghastly, gaunt, and ominous bird of yore

        Meant in croaking "Nevermore."

This I sat engaged in guessing, but no syllable expressing

To the fowl whose fiery eyes now burned into my bosom's core;

75 This and more I sat divining, with my head at ease reclining

On the cushion's velvet lining that the lamplight gloated o'er,

But whose velvet-violet lining with the lamplight gloating o'er,

        She shall press, ah, nevermore!

Then, methought, the air grew denser, perfumed from an unseen censer

80 Swung by seraphim° whose footfalls tinkled on the tufted floor.

"Wretch," I cried, "thy God hath lent thee—by these angels he hath sent thee

Respite—respite and nepenthe° from thy memories of Lenore;

Quaff, oh quaff this kind nepenthe and forget this lost Lenore!"

        Quoth the Raven "Nevermore."

85 "Prophet!" said I, "thing of evil!—prophet still, if bird or devil!

Whether Tempter sent, or whether tempest tossed thee here ashore,

Desolate yet all undaunted, on this desert land enchanted—

On this home by Horror haunted—tell me truly, I implore—

Is there—*is* there balm in Gilead?°—tell me—tell me, I implore!"

90   Quoth the Raven "Nevermore."

---

80. seraphim: the highest of the nine ranks of angels.

82. nepenthe: a sleeping potion which people long ago believed would relieve pain and sorrow.

89. Is there balm in Gilead?: a line from the Bible meaning *Is there any relief from my sorrow?*

"Prophet!" said I, "thing oft evil!—prophet still, if bird or devil!
By that Heaven that bends above us—by that God we both adore—
Tell this soul with sorrow laden if, within the distant Aidenn,
It shall clasp a sainted maiden whom the angels name Lenore—
95   Clasp a rare and radiant maiden whom the angels name Lenore."
        Quoth the Raven "Nevermore."

"Be that word our sign of parting, bird or fiend!" I shrieked,
        upstarting—
"Get thee back into the tempest and the Night's Plutonian shore!
Leave no black plume as a token of that lie thy soul hath spoken!
100   Leave my loneliness unbroken!—quit the bust above my door!
Take thy beak from out my heart, and take thy form from off my
        door!"
        Quoth the Raven "Nevermore."

And the Raven, never flitting, still is sitting, *still* is sitting
On the pallid bust of Pallas just above my chamber door;
105   And his eyes have all the seeming of a demon's that is dreaming,
And the lamplight o'er him streaming throws his shadow on the
        floor;
And my soul from out that shadow that lies floating on the floor
        Shall be lifted—nevermore!

Am I on Track?

Actual Time Spent Reading

Poe's Process:
Writing "The Raven"

Many years ago after the hugely successful publication of "The Raven," Poe wrote an essay describing how he composed it. He described the writing of the poem as though he were solving a mathematical puzzle. Here are some of the first steps in Poe's writing process:

1. He decided he wanted to write a poem with a melancholy effect.

2. Then he decided that the melancholy would be reinforced by the refrain "Nevermore" (he liked its sound) and that a raven would utter the refrain. (Before he settled on a raven, though, he considered other birds for the part.)

10

3. Finally, he decided his subject would be what he thought was the most melancholy subject in the world: a lover mourning for a beautiful woman who has died.

Now Poe was ready to write. The first stanza he wrote, he claimed, was the climactic one, lines 85–90. From there he set about choosing his details: the interior space in which the lover, who is a student, and the raven are brought together; the tapping that introduces the raven; the fact that the night is stormy rather than calm; and the action of the raven alighting on the bust of Pallas.

20

Then Poe goes on to describe his writing process:

"The raven addressed, answers with its customary word, 'Nevermore'—a word which finds immediate echo in the melancholy heart of the student, who, giving utterance aloud to certain thoughts suggested by the occasion, is again startled by the fowl's repetition of 'Nevermore.'

NOTES

"The student now guesses the state of the case, but is impelled, as I have before explained, by the human thirst for self-torture, and in part by superstition, to propound such queries to the bird as will bring him, the lover, the most of the luxury of sorrow, through the anticipated answer 'Nevermore.' . . .

"It will be observed that the words 'from out my heart' involve the first metaphorical expression in the poem. They, with the answer 'Nevermore,' dispose the mind to seek a moral in all that has been previously narrated. The reader begins now to regard the raven as emblematical [symbolic]—but it is not until the very last line of the very last stanza, that the intention of making him emblematical of *Mournful and never ending Remembrance* is permitted distinctly to be seen. . . ."

Part 1 Questions

Answer the following questions. You may refer to your reading notes, and you should cite text evidence in your responses. Your answers to these questions will be scored. You will be able to refer to your answers as you write your essay in Part 2.

1 Which word from the following lines of text in Source #2 helps you understand the meaning of *discourse*?

> Much I marveled this ungainly fowl to hear discourse so plainly,
> Though its answer little meaning—little relevancy bore;
> For we cannot help agreeing that no living human being
> Ever yet was blessed with seeing bird above his chamber door—
> (lines 49–52)

  a. fowl

  b. answer

  c. relevancy

  d. agreeing

2 Which of the following sentences best explains Poe's purpose in composing "The Raven," as described in Source #3?

  a. He wanted to write a poem about the defeat of despair.

  b. He wanted to show that the repetition of a single word could drive someone mad.

  c. He wanted the ending of the poem to surprise the reader by providing a single, calculated effect.

  d. He wanted to write a melancholy poem about loss.

3 Select three pieces of evidence from "The Raven" that **best** support your answer to Question 3.

a. "Once upon a midnight dreary, while I pondered, weak and weary . . ." (line 1)

b. " 'Tis some visitor,' I muttered, 'tapping at my chamber door—'" (line 5)

c. " . . . vainly I had sought to borrow / From my books surcease of sorrow— sorrow for the lost Lenore—" (lines 9–10)

d. "'Let my heart be still a moment and this mystery explore;— / 'Tis the wind and nothing more!'" (lines 35–36)

e. "In there stepped a stately Raven of the saintly days of yore . . . " (line 38)

f. " . . . 'Other friends have flown before— / On the morrow *he* will leave me, as my Hopes have flown before.' / Then the bird said 'Nevermore.'" (lines 58–60)

g. "This I sat engaged in guessing, but no syllable expressing / To the fowl whose fiery eyes now burned into my bosom's core . . . " (lines 73–74)

h. "'Tell this soul with sorrow laden if, within the distant Aidenn, / It shall clasp a sainted maiden whom the angels name Lenore— / Clasp a rare and radiant maiden whom the angels name Lenore.' / Quoth the Raven 'Nevermore.'" (lines 93–96)

4 **Prose Constructed-Response** Write a paragraph explaining how "The Raven" displays Poe's interest in the "dark, irrational depths of the human mind" (Source #1, lines 7–8). Cite evidence from the sources to support your response.

_____

_____

_____

_____

_____

_____

_____

_____

_____

_____

_____

_____

▶ Part 2 (85 minutes)

You will have 85 minutes to review your notes and sources, plan, draft, edit, and revise your essay. While you may use your notes and refer to the sources, your essay must represent your original work. You may refer to your responses to Part 1, but you cannot change those answers. Now read your assignment and the information about how your writing will be scored; then begin your work.

Your Assignment

The deadline for the essay contest is approaching, and it is time to start writing your analysis of the representation of the "human thirst for self-torture" in Poe's poem "The Raven." When writing your analysis, make sure to support your ideas with evidence from the sources. Remember to present your ideas in a logical order.

Literary Analysis Scoring

Your literary analysis will be scored using the following:

1. **Organization/purpose:** How well did you state your thesis/controlling idea and support it with a logical progression of ideas? Did you use a variety of transitions between ideas? Was your controlling idea narrow enough to lead to a logical conclusion?

2. **Evidence/elaboration:** How well did you incorporate relevant information from the literary texts? How well did you elaborate your ideas? Did you use precise language appropriate to your audience and purpose?

3. **Conventions:** How well did you follow the rules of grammar, punctuation, capitalization, and spelling?

Now begin work on your literary analysis. Manage your time carefully so that you can:

- plan your essay, using your notes
- write your essay
- revise and edit your final draft

Acknowledgments

"Fifteen" from *The Way It Is: New and Selected Poems* by William Stafford. Text copyright © 1966, 1998 by the Estate of William Stafford. Reprinted by permission of the Permissions Company on behalf of the Estate of William Stafford and Graywolf Press.

"Kipling and I" by Jesús Colón from *Growing Up Latino: Memoirs and Stories,* edited by Harold Augenbraum and Ilan Stavans. Text copyright © 1993 by Harold Augenbraum and Ilan Stavans. Reprinted by permission of International Publishers.

Excerpt from "Regulations Do Change Eating Behavior" by Marion Nestle from *SFGate,* August 31, 2012, www.sfgate.com. Text copyright © 2012 by Marion Nestle. Reprinted by permission of Lydia Wills LLC on behalf of Marion Nestle.

"School Start Time and Sleep" from *The National Sleep Foundation,* www.sleepfoundation.org. Text copyright © 2011 by The National Sleep Foundation. Reprinted by permission of The National Sleep Foundation.

Excerpt from "Soda-Size Cap is a Public Health Issue" (Retitled: "Food Politics") by Marion Nestle from *SFGate,* February 1, 2013, www.sfgate. com. Text copyright © 2013 by Marion Nestle. Reprinted by permission of Lydia Wills LLC on behalf of Marion Nestle.

"Sugary Drinks Over 16-Ounces Banned in New York City, Board of Health Votes" by Ryan Jaslow from *CBS News,* September 13, 2012, www. cbsnews.com. Text copyright © 2012 by CBS Broadcasting, Inc. Reprinted by permission of CBS Broadcasting, Inc.

"Teenage Driving Laws May Just Delay Deadly Crashes" by Anahad O'Connor from *The New York Times,* September 14, 2011. Text copyright © 2011 by The New York Times. Reprinted by permission of PARS International on behalf of The New York Times.